T0197126

Richard Rayner

DRAKE'S FORTUNE

Richard Rayner is the author of several books, including the novel *The Cloud Sketcher* and *The Blue Suit*, a memoir of his own life as a thief while a student at Cambridge University. His work appears in *The New Yorker*, *The New York Times*, the *Los Angeles Times*, and other publications. He lives with his family in Los Angeles.

DRAKE'S FORTUNE

DRAKE'S FORTUNE

The Fabulous True Story of

the World's Greatest

Confidence Artist

Richard Rayner

ANCHOR BOOKS

A Division of Random House, Inc.

New York

FIRST ANCHOR BOOKS EDITION, OCTOBER 2003

Copyright © 2002 by Richard Rayner

All rights reserved under International and Pan-American Copyright
Conventions. Published in the United States by Anchor Books, a division
of Random House, Inc., New York, and simultaneously in Canada
by Random House of Canada Limited, Toronto. Originally published
in hardcover in the United States by Doubleday, a division of
Random House, Inc., New York, in 2002.

Anchor Books and colophon are registered
trademarks of Random House, Inc.

The Library of Congress has cataloged the Doubleday edition as follows:
Rayner, Richard, 1955–
Drake's fortune : the fabulous true story of the world's greatest
confidence artist / Richard Rayner.—1st ed.
p. cm.
Includes index.
ISBN 0-385-49949-3
1. Hartzell, Oscar Merrill, 1876–1943.
2. Swindlers and swindling—United States—Biography. I. Title.
HV6692.H37 A3 2002
364.1'36'092—dc21
[B]
2001052981

Anchor ISBN: 978-0-385-49950-7

Author photograph © Jerry Bauer
Book design by Dana Leigh Treglia

www.anchorbooks.com

For Paivi and Harry

and Charlie

CONTENTS

"All that deceives may be said to enchant."
—*Plato*

"I ain't done nothing wouldn't nobody do if they had a chance to make a pile of money."
—*Chester Himes*

DRAKE'S FORTUNE

PROLOGUE

Nineteen thirty-three was the height of the Great Depression, an abysmal time. The gaudy spree of the Jazz Age was just a memory, and throughout the world huge numbers of people found themselves condemned to destitution, misery, and despair. In America, Franklin Roosevelt had only recently become president and more than ten million were still out of work. Armies of migrants—homeless, jobless—roamed the country, fighting to survive. More than three thousand banks had closed since the Wall Street crash of 1929. A blues song of the era declared: "Lord, I'm so low down, baby/I declare I'm looking up at down."

America's farmers were especially hard hit. More than a quarter of them had already lost their lands, and the agrarian state of Iowa was in open revolt. Taking their shotguns, their pitchforks, their reaper blades, striking Iowa farmers barricaded roads outside Sioux City and other market towns. They stopped milk and hay wagons and overturned trucks that tried to cross their picket lines. The aim was to stop produce from getting to market and drive prices back up to an acceptable level. Outnumbered law enforcement officers had their pistols snatched away from them. Imprisoned heroes of the farmers' union were busted out of jail. Agents of the loathed banks and insurance companies were threatened and intimidated. A judge was kidnapped, hanged until he was almost dead, and made to kiss the American flag—because he'd been trying to enforce an enclosure order.

Faith in the established order had vanished, and there were reasons. In some places the price of corn was minus three cents a bushel—if a farmer wanted to sell a bushel he had to bring in three cents. The farmers were frightened and angry, yet these were conservative men who still believed in democracy and the ideals of America; they wanted to work, to live in peace while they supported their families and accrued wealth. They weren't looking for revolution; they were looking for hope.

An eyewitness remembered that the situation in Iowa was so tense you could almost smell the gunpowder. Into this atmosphere arrived an extraordinary figure, a man in a derby hat smoking a cigar, a fifty-seven-year-old man with a vast steamship trunk full of silk shirts and costly suits custom-tailored on London's Savile Row, a heavyset man with a ruddy, jowly face and a smile that demanded trust. His name was Oscar Hartzell. He dressed like a wealthy banker, indeed like one of the mistrusted Wall Street men, but he'd once farmed in the area and spoke a language the Siouxlanders understood. He had a rough charm and was always ready with a slap on the back or a cigar for his friends. He had a winning salesman's personality and was greeted by thousands of humbled Iowa folk like a returning conqueror, like a savior. They followed him and believed in him with a respect bordering on awe, worship. And yet he'd stolen millions of dollars from them.

Until recently, Hartzell had been living in England, but now he'd been fetched back to Sioux City to face a multitude of charges of fraud and misuse of the mails. Another local man, Harry Reed, a U.S. attorney from the nearby city of Waterloo, had the job of securing the conviction, bringing this rascal to justice. At first Reed saw this as a simple matter, for he knew Hartzell to be the biggest confidence trickster of an era that scarcely lacked for them, an artful dodger who in London had restyled himself as a British lord and financed a decade of luxury and high living by swindling between 70,000 and 100,000 Midwesterners.

Things weren't going according to plan, however. As the trial began, prosecutor Harry Reed found himself jostled and spat upon, while the crook Oscar Hartzell was lionized and cheered and borne shoulder-high by supporters who steadfastly refused to accept that he was a con man. They believed him their economic redeemer, a man of the people who any day now would turn them all into millionaires. He would lead them out of the swamps of the Depression and toward the banquet table of the Lord. He would lay before them the greatest aggregate of wealth in the world and create an entire new social order. He would do this by delivering into their hands the estate of the Elizabethan sea rover Sir Francis Drake, an accumulation of cash, lands, investments, jewels, gold, gems, and other treasures now worth more than $100 billion. They would all be rich—rich! Governments would topple, the world's economy would be turned upside down as if in a doomed socialite's cocktail shaker, and Hartzell would emerge in his true colors as a figure of unknown and unspeakable power.

Harry Reed met hundreds of decent people who'd been taken by Hartzell, yet not one of them was prepared to speak against him. Afflicted by delusion or mania, they besieged the federal courthouse in Sioux City and threatened to turn the trial into a circus. They were suckers who had no wish to be saved, even from themselves, and Reed, bewildered, wasn't sure whether he'd stumbled across a strange hybrid of religious revivalism or into the pages of some fantastic novel. At the center of it all was Oscar Hartzell, grinning like a benign patriarch, a huckster, a charmer, a pied piper who wore an English-style pince-nez attached on a loop to his breast pocket and assured his devoted followers he would soon be more powerful than

Roosevelt, than Hitler, than Mussolini, and then the world's greatest wealth would all be theirs.

⟶·

I first came across the story of Oscar Hartzell in Jay Robert Nash's book *Hustlers and Con Men*, an anecdotal history of swindles down the ages, a compendium of the grift. The back cover had a photograph of Nash, a Chicago journalist and entrepreneur (himself something of a Gatsby figure), leaning forward with an impish smile to light a cigarette for Joseph "Yellow Kid" Weil, the most famous American con man of all, the model for the Robert Redford character in the movie *The Sting*. The pages within showed Nash going about his work with similar pep and gusto. He told how Wall Street's Daniel Drew got his start by selling bloated cows to Henry Astor; how Jay Gould and Big Jim Fisk conned Commodore Cornelius Vanderbilt into trying to corner the market in shares in the Erie Railroad and relieved him of a fortune by simply pumping out more and more stock, thus making the market uncornerable; how Wilson Mizner, an ace deepwater sharper, worked a multitude of scams to fleece the prosperous on the decks of the early transatlantic steamships; how Philip Arnold and John Slack made a fortune by salting a fake diamond mine and sending San Francisco into a frenzy in 1871; how the Spanish prisoner game, with its call to easy adventure through the promise of an easy fortune and a beautiful girl, keeps popping up every decade or so; how Yellow Kid Weil sold a string of mutts from the Chicago city pound as though they were priceless pedigree dogs. And so on: Nash told of the systems behind medical frauds, stock frauds, magazine sales frauds, and other rackets with evocative names like the tat, the wire, the big store.

In time I discovered that books on con artistry can easily be viewed through the wrong end of the telescope. That's to say, they lend themselves to consideration as how-to manuals and not only warnings or story anthologies. This is true from J. P. Johnston's *Grafters I Have Met* (1906) to Charles R. Whitlock's *Chuck Whitlock's Scam School* (1997). David Maurer's classic study *The Big Con* (1941) later so impressed the people at Universal that they lifted the plot of *The Sting* from it and had to settle with the Maurer estate to the tune of $800,000. *Hustlers and Con Men* (1976) was no exception to this perennial trend; it read like the flip side of the other sort of American self-help manual, the ones that point a more legitimate road to happiness and success, those written by, say, Dale Carnegie and, more recently, Anthony Robbins. Nash invited his reader to awake the swindler within, and I began to wonder whether the confidence man might in fact be the great covert, or not so covert, American hero.

In the fifth chapter of *Hustlers and Con Men*, entitled "The Inherited Billions," I found ten or so pages about Oscar Hartzell. In Nash's telling he was an Iowa farm boy who became a con man, lived like a king off the Drake Estate in London in the 1920s and early 1930s, was caught, and finally died mad—or perhaps not—in the Medical Center for Federal Prisoners at Springfield, Missouri, on August 27, 1943. Nash wrote:

> When Oscar Hartzell arrived in London, he posed as an oil-rich Texas millionaire and promptly discarded his country bumpkin style. He rented a luxurious suite of rooms on London's fashionable Basil Street and immediately had a hundred suits meticulously tailored by the finest haberdashers along Saville [sic] Row. Only the best restaurants sufficed for his daily meals, and season tickets to the most important shows were habitually tucked into his vest pockets. Wenching became a

devout pastime for Oscar until he caused one buxom blonde barmaid to get in the family way. Her father showed up at his rooms and remonstrated with Oscar to "do the right thing." Hartzell not only turned on the back country charm but let loose his herculean pitch, convincing the Cockney father of his fabulous Drake heir story to the point where the old man rushed to the bank, withdrew his savings, and invested $2,600 in the scheme. Oscar then stopped seeing the girl.

This paragraph was jaunty, even irresistible, but somehow reality escaped it; already the writing seemed too broad, too much the movie version. A hundred Savile Row suits? A buxom blond barmaid? What drew me in was the outline of such an extravagant and complete story, the suggestion of a man's whole life driven and defined by one outrageous imposture. The sheer longevity of the con was startling. How had Hartzell kept it going for so long? Nash's account, based on previously published newspaper and magazine sources, had obvious holes, and I wondered what might exist in the way of letters, court records, police reports, psychiatric evaluations, and other documentation. My own father had been a con man, and I knew from personal experience that such a life creates more legal and emotional residue than Nash, for the purposes of his book, had needed to contemplate. I had a hunch that a fuller investigation would reveal unguessed-at twists and turns.

And so a three-year quest began. It led me to the birthplace of a legendary lawman and gunslinger (Hartzell's birthplace too), to the covered bridges of Madison County, to courtrooms in Sioux City and Chicago, to the handsome old port of Plymouth and the plains of Minnesota, to apartments in seedy West London and ritzy Knightsbridge. Along the way I visited scores of different libraries and offices of records, filling in a more complete picture of Oscar

Hartzell. In the U.S. National Archive in College Park, Maryland, in a cellophane folder, slipped to the bottom of a file box so that I almost missed it, typed on yellowed paper that was brittle and crumbling to the touch, I made the most extraordinary find of all—Hartzell's incomplete autobiography, a testament no one else had read in more than sixty-five years. It was as if he'd walked through the door to take me by the hand.

There are, of course, many contenders for the title of best American swindler, but Hartzell has a good claim, I think; I set out to unearth his story, and it proved to be a more fabulous saga than any fabulist could dare to imagine.

⌣

The story really begins in 1572 when King Philip II of Spain was the most powerful monarch on earth. An unsung English seaman named Francis Drake led a small expedition to the isthmus of Panama, attacking shipping and coastal settlements and even venturing inland to search for the mule trains that hauled Spanish Peruvian treasure from the Pacific Coast to Nombre de Dios.

Drake was the son of a yeoman farmer. No record remains of the date of his birth, but it was sometime between 1541 and 1545, which means that in 1572 he was in his late twenties or early thirties. Bearded, stocky, and strong, slightly florid in the face, he was known to be cheerful in misfortune and charitable in success. Drake was already developing the talent for which history would come to know him—a knack for lifting and leading men; he was also vain, ambitious, and possessed of a self-confidence and belief in his own powers that seemed at times to transcend sanity.

Drake's first two attacks failed; his men were struck by fever and disease, and further skirmishes reduced their number. But then, in alliance with the French captain Guillaume Le Testu and a party of escaped black slaves, he surprised a train of mules carrying treasure so close to the port of Nombre de Dios that he and his men could hear the hammers of the blacksmiths as they worked on the Spanish fleet. Quickly the attackers struck and hauled off a quantity of gold bullion, its value later to be estimated at 100,000 gold pesos, approximately 40,000 pounds sterling in Elizabethan money, a fortune in today's terms. Le Testu, hurt and unable to move, was left behind. The Spaniards showed no mercy, for at this moment Spain was at war with neither England nor France and in King Philip's eyes Drake and his band were nothing more than pirates, thieves who, should they happen to be caught, fully deserved a blade across the throat.

For Queen Elizabeth the privateers were a tool for expanding England's commercial future and her own financial interests. She kept secret her part in these expeditions, but since Drake had made a success of this one she sanctioned another, and in December 1577 he set out again from Plymouth, this time with four ships, well armed and well equipped. Among the backers were the Earl of Leicester, Sir Francis Walsyngham, and the queen herself, who put up £1,000 on the sly. The one surviving copy of Drake's instructions envisages a trading voyage, but this was just a blind to throw off the Spanish should the document fall into their hands. The true goal was plunder. Drake hoped to surprise a treasure ship and return home in pomp with the booty.

What started as blunt privateering became the first British circumnavigation of the globe, one of sailing's epic feats. Drake's squadron passed through the equatorial doldrums, rounded Cape Horn amid fearful storms, and struck land for a refit in an area of what we now call northern California, which Drake promptly claimed for the English and dubbed New Albion. Along the way, off the Pacific coast of Peru (unprotected by the Spaniards, who had considered an attack from this side impossible), he had indeed captured a treasure ship, the *Nuestra Señora de la Concepción*, laden with gold pesos, silver, pearls, silks, damasks, spices, and other treasures such as dreams are made of.

Drake crossed the Pacific in the belt of the northeast trade winds and was twice almost sunk in the Indian Ocean before rounding the Cape of Good Hope and passing once again into the more familiar waters of the Atlantic. He arrived back in Plymouth almost two years after he set out, having gathered so much plunder he feared that Spain might start a war over it, or that the queen might arrest or even behead him. The Spaniards were calling for the pirate Drake—El Draque, the Dragon, as they called him—to be handed over for summary execution. Instead, Elizabeth didn't even wait for Drake's flagship, the *Golden Hind*, to enter port, but went out to the ship, knighted Drake, and took off for London with the swag.

For its investors this expedition yielded a fabulous return of 4,700 percent, not including the bonuses that were set aside for Drake and the queen. Some said that Elizabeth got more than she should have, that in effect she stole some of the booty, but who was to argue? She took £100,000. It's hard to give contemporary meaning to this sum, but at that time £100,000 would have bought 4 million days of skilled labor—here was a staggering amount of money, in other words, perhaps more than $1 billion today. With it Elizabeth laid the foundations of a foreign investment fortune, and England began to grow into a world colonial power. With his own share, Drake bought a large country seat, the stately Buckland Abbey near Plymouth, and set about obliterating once and for all his humble origins. In his quest to turn himself into a gentleman he applied for a coat of arms, the ultimate badge of English aristocratic swagger.

Nothing quite appals the English like new money, especially when those who are being appalled have had theirs only a generation or two, and many surrounding Elizabeth at court saw in Drake only a jumped-up braggart, flaunting his new prestige like a peacock. For the commoners, however, who worked the farms or plied their trades in the filthy London streets and then drank in the taverns or crammed the pit of the Swan Theater to see the latest entertainments by Christopher Marlowe and William Shakespeare, Drake was more than merely a beloved hero, a man risen to eminence through bravery and remarkable deeds. He was already an almost mythical figure, an individual who, it often seemed, was waging a personal war on behalf of his queen against the world's most powerful empire. Pamphlets and broadsheets tracked his actions. Sometimes he was wrongly reported killed, or wounded, or captured; more often he was said to be wreaking havoc, "singeing the king of Spain's beard."

Drake was instrumental in defeating the Spanish Armada in 1588, when (notably, coolly, perhaps apocryphally) he refused to go to sea until he'd finished his game of bowls. Old and wealthy enough to have retired, he died at sea off Panama, trying to wrest yet more loot from the Spaniards for himself and the queen he adored. The date was January 28, 1596.

Some lives are more remarkable than others. Some are so shapely, so seemingly structured and packed with meaning, that the imagination at once strikes sparks off them. Sir Francis Drake's was such a life. He died famous, he died as—for the latter part of his life—he'd lived, a figure of legend to whom improbable and sometimes even true stories clung like dust to an Elizabethan silk ruff. He died rich and he died, despite having been married twice, without children. Most of his land and money went to his brother and his nephews.

When, within a few years of Drake's death, the standards of the English navy slipped, it was natural for there to be a demand for a return to the glories of the recent past; the campaign was called Sir Francis Drake Revived. Equally, it was unsurprising, given that Drake left no direct heir, when fortune hunters proclaimed there had been something untoward with his will, something fishy about it—the will had been forged, they claimed, or in any event had been wrongly probated and was invalid. Vast wealth was there for the taking, they said, for him who could untangle the legal knot.

The English navy was duly set straight and embarked on three centuries of oceanic dominance. But while Britannia was ruling the waves, the legend of Sir Francis Drake's will, and the wealth that was locked up in probate, never quite went away. It persisted in England and took hold and flourished in America too when some of Drake's relatives emigrated there, settling in Virginia, Ohio, Iowa, Illinois, and Missouri. In 1884, James Russell Lowell, American ambassador to London, had to draw up a form letter to answer the steady stream of inquiries from his credulous countrymen asking about the fortune. In 1892 his successor to the London posting, Robert Todd Lincoln, son of the president who had once said, "You can fool some of the people all of the time," issued a statement warning prospective investors against "putting any money with persons claiming to have any interest in any so-called Sir Francis Drake Estate."

Confidence tricks are born but they never die. They flourish, fade, and then spring back to life in new clothes. They're stories, and, like stories, they stick to effective formulas. The unclaimed estate swindle is one of the oldest forms of con, and it was enjoying a particular vogue in America at the end of the nineteenth century. Belief blossomed in the existence of the Drake Estate and a multitude of other fictitious inheritances such as the Jennens (or Jennings or Jannens), the Hedges, the Baker, the Bradford, the Hyde, the Horne, the Townley, the Mosher, the Weber (or Webber), the Nixon, the Bogardus, the Kern, the Cronkheit, the DuBois, the Wertz (or Wirtz or Wurtz). People in Illinois and California spoke about when they would get their hands on the Blake millions, or the castles and fisheries of the Duke of Argyle. In New York there were those ready to be convinced by con men that the Trinity Church Corporation falsely held its vast properties on Wall Street and elsewhere. But the majority of these estates were said to exist in Europe. The promoters grasped that with the passage of time the wealth of the Old World had taken on a romantic otherness. Perhaps treasure really was buried back there.

The estate schemes touched the democratic suspicion that inherited wealth is fortuitous and arbitrary and deserved by anybody as much as anybody else; they called upon the yearning for that polish of class which history and tradition are said to bring; they tapped into a beginning obsession with genealogy.

The next phase of the Drake swindle owed its arrival to a scientific development, the telephone, and its commercial and social offshoot the telephone directory. In 1900 a gang of swindlers collected the names of all the Drakes they could find in the American directories and sent out wires, informing them that they were legitimate heirs. A few days later these lucky beneficiaries received letters from a supposed firm of London solicitors, confirming their claim, but asking for a fee to clear up the final stages of the litigation. By this time many of the dupes were convinced. Their pictures appeared in hometown and even metropolitan papers and they were congratulated by proud and expectant friends. On June 18, 1903, the *Journal Gazette* of Logan, Ohio, ran the following article:

HEIRS WILL CONTEST PROPERTY
WORTH MILLIONS
Representatives Who Went to London for Ohio Heirs Tell the Story

The heirs of that great sea rover Sir Francis Drake in the United States are getting active for the recovery of a large estate in England. Descendants of Drake in Morgan County recently sent an attorney to England to look after their interests. The report is of local interest as many of the descendants reside in Logan and Hocking County. The Bowen family of this city are descendants of England's annihilator of the dreaded Armada and Capt. William F. Bowen has much data of genealogical interest and otherwise bearing on the case.

Mr. James Drake of McConnelsville, and Attorney L. C. Russel of Newark, returned Sunday from England where they have been looking up the interests of the Drake heirs in the Sir Francis Drake estate.

On the 29th or in 11 days they arrived in Liverpool. The following day they left by train for London and crossed the great but small kingdom in four hours. Think of the relative size of the United States and England. It requires 30 times as long to cross our country. The next day May 31st they went 190 miles south from London toward the English Channel to Exeter, near where the famous Drake mansion and estate is.

They found the facts to be briefly as follows: Sir Francis Drake died in 1595, leaving one of the finest estates in England. By the will and the English laws it passed to the oldest son and son on down the line forever until some descendant died without male heir when the property was to be divided among all the heirs of the original owner. Francis Henry Drake the 5th baron in line, died in 1795 without male heir but willed his property to his daughters without regard to former ancestral requirements. This will is pronounced fraudulent, and the possession of the property since by the descendants has been illegal. The property is now held by Lady Elliot Drake, one of the leaders of the English aristocracy. Mr. James Drake and his attorney Mr. Russel retained an English lawyer at Exeter to investigate the matter and he will have an expert genealogist trace the descent of the original owners to establish the claims of the American heirs when suit will be instituted to recover the property.

Confusions and inaccuracies abound here, but what's interesting is the matter-of-fact tone, the straightforward and uninflected style of the reporting. The apparent situation is presented clearly and without hint of irony or spin: an error has been detected, a suit will be filed, and the error will be corrected. According to the *Journal Gazette*, bad luck is about to descend upon poor Lady Drake, who will have to give up everything she owns, even though she is a "leader of the English aristocracy." Notably, it's as if the warnings of Lowell and Lincoln had never been issued; they'd already been forgotten, or were being ignored.

During the next years the editors of the *Journal Gazette* kept their eye on the progress of the case. Legal technicalities preventing settlement came up year after year with monotonous regularity. Prospective heirs spent thousands of dollars in the contest. Other heirs from other cities in Ohio and from other states, represented by other promoters and their lawyers, popped up to stake their claim. The important idea of rival heirs was introduced, but the fundamental premise, the proposition that the Drake Estate was for real and could be delivered by *somebody*, was never questioned.

In December 1906 the *Ohio State Journal* asked:

WILL THE ESTATE OF SIR FRANCIS DRAKE NOTED PIRATE AND FIRST ENGLISH ADMIRAL DESCEND TO A COLUMBUS MAN?

M. A. Glenn of 946 east Long Street, who declares that he has proved himself to be a descendant of the great Sir Francis, has received word from England that the Drake estate has been ordered released by Court of Chancery and that a division is soon to take place. The estate is worth millions. English attorneys, says Mr. Glenn, have computed its actual value at $250,000,000. It is mainly in jewels and money and has been held for years by the Bank of England. Interest has augmented it.

It must have seemed, even to the most optimistic of con men, that this sweet game couldn't last; in fact, its great maverick had yet to sit down at the table.

ONE

The Education of a Con Man

Oscar Merrill Hartzell was a son of the prairie, of the American heartland, of Monmouth, a small city (even today the population is only nine thousand) in western Illinois that Abraham Lincoln visited often during the early years of his legal career. Wyatt Earp was born there in 1848, and it's where Ronald Reagan attended second grade in 1918. Hartzell, whose life would in its own way be as emblematically American, was born there on January 6, 1876.

One of his grandfathers was a steamboat man. His father, John Henry Hartzell, came originally from Tiltensville, Ohio, but moved west when he was eighteen to work as a hired hand for Eliza Jane Shaw, a widow who had a farm outside Monmouth. John Henry Hartzell was quarrelsome and hot-tempered, but a hard worker, a capable farmer, and evidently a man who, even if he allowed one eye to stray in the direction of love, always kept the other fixed firmly on the main chance. On Christmas Day 1874, he married one of Eliza Jane Shaw's daughters, and with his wedding gift he bought his own small holding of twenty acres.

Oscar, their first child, was born just over a year later in the one-room log cabin that John Hartzell had raised with his own hands. A daughter, Pearl May, soon followed, and then Emma Hartzell lost her third pregnancy during childbirth. The next child was yet another boy, Clinton, but here arises a confusion. Some records suggest that he was a natural birth, but Oscar would one day claim that Clinton was adopted. (Of this important divergence, more later.)

The family was completed by the birth of Canfield, Oscar's youngest brother, in 1880.

John Hartzell, the patriarch, was stable, steady, strict, a Protestant of German descent who lived a gospel of hard work and grasping thrift. Emma Hartzell was subsequently described as "the sweet, motherly type usually relied upon to guide her offspring in righteous paths." Unlike her husband, she was patient and indulgent, always ready to help Oscar with his homework (he was poor at grammar) or to press a cold cloth to his forehead if he had a headache. As a child he suffered from the usual ailments—measles, mumps, chickenpox—but was otherwise a healthy and robust boy. He was active and intelligent and considered of unusual promise.

John Hartzell added to his land until he had more than four hundred acres and then built a new nine-room house. Oscar's room on the upper story had a view of the prairie. On his entry to the local country school in Cold Creek, his future seemed to be already written—he would follow his father, be a farmer. Oscar milked the cows before breakfast; he learned how to pierce the skin and bring relief to an animal that had eaten clover. When he stole a penknife at school, he was whipped for it. When he gambled, and won from his friends a pint pot full of pennies, he was whipped for it, and made to give back the pennies. When his schoolteacher said he was a born businessman who would be rich some day, his father was very proud and gave him a dollar.

Oscar left school at sixteen to work on the farm. His father taught him how to castrate bulls, fatten them, and sell them as steers—Oscar's first experience of transformation and shape-shifting. His mother gave him a gold watch on his eighteenth birthday, for not chewing tobacco, and when John Hartzell took the rest of the family to the great Chicago World's Fair of 1893, Oscar opted instead to stay at home and look after the farm. As reward for this sacrifice he received a new buggy and a new riding harness; the buggy alone cost $80. "I think no one could have been more proud than I was. I went hell-for-leather over sense, riding that buggy like a madman twixt the farm and Monmouth," he wrote in his autobiography.

This typical Western childhood even had its archetypal feud: the hard-nosed John Hartzell brought lawsuits against members of his wife's family to secure her share of her grandfather's will. "There was bitter feeling and father was never without his six shooter for years. Sometimes they would set his barns on fire and I would stay out all night with my father watching the grain stacks until the threshing was done," Oscar wrote. "They were jealous of father's success. Father always made money and they did not know how to make money."

It was a time in America when success was a magic word. Every small town had its story of the boy who rose from humble origins to achieve wealth and power. Such life ascents were already starting to be known as Horatio Alger stories, after the writer whose books embodied this ethos and were achieving huge popularity just at the time Oscar was growing up. His father had done very well for himself; the son intended to emulate and surpass him.

His sister, Pearl, later remembered that he was a leader and his leadership qualities were accepted. Further, he was "the outstanding boy of the community who went out with the best girls." For two years, in the quaint terminology of the time, Oscar "kept company" with Daisy Rees, from nearby Gerlaw. Daisy was the daughter of Michael Rees, a man who'd seen action with the 102nd Illinois Volunteers in the Civil War and was one of the most active and prosperous farmers in the area. Daisy was a catch, in other words, and Oscar married her beneath an arch of evergreen and chrysanthemums in the parlor of her parents' house on November 20, 1895. Daisy was lovely, her cream henrietta trimmed with satin and silk. Oscar wore the conventional black frock coat as though he wished he could burst out of it. "The groom is an industrious, energetic young farmer, and the bride a most charming young lady, loved by a large circle of friends," the *Monmouth Daily Review* reported. The marriage, which started so idyllically, was not to be a happy one.

At first the newlyweds lived in a room at the Hartzell place, but Oscar was now ready to strike out on his own, and he approached the matter as he rode his buggy—going hell for leather, doing business fast. First he rented his father's farm, then bought one, then got another, of two hundred acres, which he soon sold at a profit so that he could purchase 1,080 acres in Iowa, sixteen miles south of Des Moines.

This was a momentous and ultimately disastrous move, though it seemed natural enough; at that time, in that part of the world, any ambitious young man's compass tended to be set west. Real estate was cheap, the law was scarcely applied, you could get lost in the country and live free. Hartzell would always say the names of these places cowboy-fashion, so that Iowa became Ioway, and both s's were pronounced in Des Moines. He and Daisy had their farm in the northeast part of Madison County, where the settlers were mostly, like Hartzell himself, of German-Protestant origin. Everybody knew everybody else in this insular community. Minds were set on hard work, strong values, civic involvement, and always money; a man proved himself by how many hours he toiled in the field and how much hard cash he had in his pocket.

Oscar both fit in and didn't. Within a few years he was one of the biggest shippers of cattle and horses in the region, well known in the banks of Des Moines and around the stockyards in Chicago. Yet he was restless, fretful, and Daisy's memories of these years were unhappy; her husband was a great one for parties and dinners and drinking; he was charming with others but always nervous with her, and overanxious when making love, so their sex life was unsatisfactory. She never expected the truth if she asked a question. Oscar had a terrible temper, cursed a lot, and was rough with horses. He paced the floor of their farmhouse, chewing tobacco (the gold watch being safe in his vest pocket, he went through as much as two ten-cent plugs per day) and speaking of what they would do when they had *real* money. He was always thinking of the next thing, longing for prestige and success, dreaming of it, already tasting it. He wanted to be the biggest fellow in the country. Later, when asked to name one of her husband's best qualities, Daisy said, "He liked to help poor people." Asked if he was peculiar in any way, she said simply: "Money, money."

On August 30, 1905, Hartzell's father, John Hartzell, went hunting with friends from Monmouth. He was at the back of his buggy reloading his five-chamber .38 Colt when suddenly he exclaimed, "My God, I'm shot." His friends heard the shot and came around from the front of the buggy just as he was falling.

John Hartzell was taken to a nearby house, where a doctor operated on him, removing a bullet that had entered above the navel and passed through three intestines before striking the hipbone. While he lay in bed, struggling for life, the *Monmouth Daily Review* issued bulletins every day, sometimes twice a day, about his progress. At first things looked very bleak indeed; two weeks later, however, John Hartzell was hailed as one case in a thousand—his robust constitution having pulled him through, every sign pointed to complete recovery. Then he had a dream that made him startled and nervous. He woke up, alarmed, and demanded to be taken home. Five minutes later he was dead—the result, apparently, of an embolism in the brain. The end came almost before those present could realize it.

Thirty years on, Oscar would still talk of this event with a crack in his voice.

The postmortem, attended by ten doctors, was delayed to await the arrival of a train bringing an investigator from Chicago. John Hartzell was so heavily insured that a question mark lay over his death. Had it been a suicide? At the inquest a jury of local men stuck together and concluded that he "came to his death accidentally by a bullet fired from his own hand."

Oscar, who'd been in Chicago on business, returned to Monmouth in time to help shoulder his father's coffin. John Hartzell was laid in the ground and his estate was valued at $10,000, with the various insurance policies bringing a further $69,000, a massive sum in 1905. Oscar took his share and started thinking about Texas.

He'd met Robert Moody, a tall, dignified millionaire who wore his graying beard trimmed to a point. In his stiff black suits Moody looked like a banker, and indeed he was; but he was also a rancher and a broker who still owned a lumberyard, a meat market, and a hotel in the Texas panhandle town of Canadian in Hemphill County, where he'd worked hard for twenty years and which he'd had a large hand in creating. Earlier in his life, when he'd been starting out, Moody had met P. T. Barnum in New York, was befriended by the showman, and subsequently managed his Dipper Ranch in Colorado. One time he fought off an Apache war party while running the entire bacon stock of Kansas City down to Santa Fe. Moody reminds us that the Wild West was as much a theater for business as for settling and exploration and gunplay. By the time Hartzell encountered him he was something of a legend, living proof that the never-quit spirit would indeed bring fortune. In Canadian he hadn't needed to worry when some of his business propositions erred on the gray side of legality; he'd been the law. Yet this self-made adventurer and entrepreneur had started life as the son of a failed English baker.

Hartzell looked at Moody and was dazzled; or that's not quite right—he looked at him and saw a grander, more expansive role model than his father ever could have been. It didn't occur to him to ask whether he was made of the same stuff as Robert Moody. Instead he simply assumed that a similar success was there for the taking. Whatever Hartzell lacked, it was not confidence. He wore his bulldog manner like a suit, or cocked at the side of his mouth like one of the cigars he had started to smoke because they lent him an air of swagger.

The two men met in Kansas City sometime in 1906, when Hartzell was thirty, and Moody liked him well enough to float a proposition. Over the next year Hartzell made several journeys down to Hemphill County and then used the money from his father's insurance policy to make a down payment on a sixteen-thousand-acre ranch that was priced at $100,000. Moody nodded approval from the sidelines and fixed the mortgage.

Hartzell went into cattle shipping in a big way. In his autobiography he describes how in 1908 he and some of his cowboys were moving 850 steers and almost lost the entire herd while crossing the Canadian River. Frightened and confused by the high banks of the river at the crossing point, the cattle got as far as midstream and refused to budge.

There was one man who was about 65 years old, a very tough looking customer and he was just as tough as he looked. His nickname was River Jack and he had been brought up on the river all his life. As the steers were starting to drown River

Jack said, "I will try the last resort." I could not imagine what he was going to do and none of the rest of the boys could either. He put the spurs to his horse and found a steer on the outside of the drove with an extra long tail. He got hold of the steer's tail and took a half-hitch around the saddle horn and started with the steer, dragging him by the tail. The steer started to bawl and make a terrific howl that drew the attention of the rest of the cattle and every steer came out alive. I gave the old man a bonus of $25 when pay day came. He went to town on a spree, got drunk and into trouble, and got into jail, and I had to go bail him out. He was a very difficult character of a man to handle. A real Texas man. A frontier man.

Soon Hartzell had his own reputation. The word was that he was a cattleman on the grand scale. At the end of 1907, he claimed, he could have sold out for $500,000. He declined the offer, believing his success would only get bigger and better. He hosted parties in restaurants and bought a string of racehorses, but his prosperity was more precarious than it looked. Everything was supported by an intricate series of mortgages and loans, one propping up the next. Mark Twain once said that farming is simply a dirtier and more arduous type of gambling, roulette with cow dung. Certainly there are risks attached to the game. Hartzell was about to discover them.

In 1908 in Texas there was an outbreak of an infectious cattle virus known as the Texas itch. Herds across four counties, including Hemphill County, were quarantined and could not be shipped. By the time the epidemic was over, Hartzell's steers had lost so much weight he had to sell them at a big loss. In his autobiography he describes this in conjunction with a string of other accidents: a fire in a barn on the Iowa farm, costing him $20,000 in grain and mules; a railroad wreck that took seventeen cars of Chicago-bound cattle into a ditch; an outbreak of cholera that killed eight hundred hogs.

———

Part of the problem, and no small part of the fun, in writing about a con man is trying to figure out when he's telling the truth. In order to be successful the best con man will tend to appear to be entirely reliable, and unreliable and deceitful in only one very small but crucial area. For the swindler a reasonable portion of honesty is the best policy too, and Hartzell's autobiography is, for the most part, doggedly artless and free of intended deception. All the same, these additional mishaps (a railroad wreck?) feel like fiction. Most likely he invented them to excuse and cover the sheer shame and sorrow he felt on describing this next part of his life, the years when the world clubbed him with his failure.

What's certain is that by the middle of 1908, Hartzell was in a hole. To cover his many bank payments he hurried to Chicago and sold his Iowa cattle, some of which he'd mortgaged more than once. This was, of course, dishonest and illegal, although numbers of farmers still do it—after all, it's not so easy for banks to keep track of where cattle are, and on which ones exactly they hold a mortgage. Hartzell thought he'd covered all his obligations before the various papers came due but then learned that a Madison County banker named Simon Casady, one of those with a lien on a part of the Iowa herd, had taken offense at his sharp handling of the matter. Another local farmer, Lew Klemm, had spotted one of Casady's men trudging through Hartzell's pastures in forlorn search of the beasts that had already been sold. Perhaps Casady's man planted one of his shiny banker's shoes in some of Mark Twain's cow dung. Klemm thought this was very funny and gave Casady a hard time about it, saying the entire neighborhood had enjoyed the joke. Casady, miffed, applied the money Hartzell sent him from Chicago against another, unsecured loan, rather than against the mortgage on the cattle (which were gone), saying he could put his money wherever he damn well chose. He foreclosed on the mortgage and brought criminal charges.

Hartzell beat the criminal suit, but was forced to file for bankruptcy, and the upshot of this local tit-for-tat was a further blizzard of very expensive law. Two of the civil cases went to the Iowa Supreme Court, one to the U.S. Supreme Court itself, and Hartzell got a legal education very useful for his subsequent career. Attorneys spent the next seven years picking through the mess. Robert Moody sued Hartzell, Simon Casady sued Hartzell, and then Casady filed suit against both Robert Moody and the German Savings Bank of Des Moines, while Moody sued the bank in Kansas City, all over who had the right to get what portion of what was left of the goods and property of Oscar and Daisy Hartzell.

The very fact of the lawsuits indicated there was plenty worth fighting for. Hartzell hired the best attorneys in his neighborhood, including one, John Parsons, who was a future judge of the Supreme Court of Illinois, a man who most certainly did not work as a favor. All this cost money. The Iowa farm was valued at $84,000, the one in Texas at $110,000. Even at the knockdown rates of a bankruptcy auction the animals and personal property in Iowa went for $83,443.90. The parlor organ brought $5, and the washing machine fifty cents. Two buggies sold at $5.

Hartzell lost the lot, and the friendship of his mentor: he was not going to be a Robert Moody.

In Madison County, where hard work and thrift counted above everything, bankruptcy brought humiliation of a very public kind. A neighbor of Hartzell's went bankrupt at about this time and committed suicide; unable to see how he could go on, he hanged himself from the rafters of his barn. Hartzell was made of sterner, or more pliable, stuff. He moved to Des Moines and got himself going in a little realty business. The business went the way of the farms; it failed. In 1914 he decided to run for sheriff of Polk County on the Democratic ticket. He threw $1,500 into the campaign, but reckoned this was a good investment. The job would bring $35,000 a year, once he added in the commission he'd get on selling property under sheriff's sales. Hartzell knew the cost of everything, and was learning the value of friends in high places.

"They stole the election from me," he said much later. "I went home that night twelve hundred votes ahead and thought I was elected. The next morning they had me seventeen hundred behind."

In Iowa in 1914 there were allegations of skulduggery and crooked politics, an almost comical fracas that recalls the more recent one in Florida. "They were patent election boxes and there was something about them so they could be changed in some way. I think they discarded those machines and never used them after that. If you were an Ioway man, you probably heard of it at that time," Hartzell said.

He'd gone west and gone broke, and now he believed himself finished, washed up in Iowa. And things were bad with Daisy. She'd inherited $25,000 on her father's death but wouldn't let Oscar do what he liked with the money. This seems reasonable enough, given his track record, but he was wretched and therefore angry. These last years had seen defeat upon defeat, and he never forgave Daisy the refusal. Looking about himself, he assessed the available opportunities and realized they were few; actually, there seemed to be only one.

TWO

Crooks at War

wo characters named Sudie Whittaker and Milo Lewis must now be introduced.

Sudie Whittaker haunts this story, yet remains elusive. There is no known photograph of her. She doesn't feature in any of the available census records of the period. Newspaper reports, court testimonies, and various other documents alternately spell her name as Whittaker, Whitaker, or Whiteaker. Her first name was apparently Oseida, shortened to the more convenient Sudie, and her trail is hard to follow, although I know for sure that she'd been working the Drake con for years before Hartzell became involved, would still be working it when he disappeared from the scene, and yet was never successfully prosecuted.

"Mrs. Whittaker was very artful, capable of using the truth with greatest economy to obtain money, and a Jezebel when she got possession of it," wrote a psychiatrist who reviewed the history of the case in 1936, Jezebel being the Old Testament temptress who cold-bloodedly arranges the murder of a man whose vineyard she covets. The psychiatrist didn't claim that Sudie Whittaker was a murderer, but we see his point. She used the income from the Drake con to finance "profligate living" for herself and her family. She was a subtle and ruthless schemer, a force, a *femme fatale* whose shimmering authority impelled men to hand over their wallets.

Milo Lewis, two months younger than Hartzell, was born on March 19, 1876, just outside Dayton, Ohio. His family's origins were Welsh, and on arrival in America his father, a farmer, had settled in the East before moving to the prairie. Lewis attended grammar and high schools in Dayton and, like Hartzell, dreamed of a grander life. In 1903 he left for Chicago, the great funnel through which wheat and livestock flowed to the East, a city then dominated by its splendid skyscrapers and the stench of its gargantuan abattoirs. Chicago was blunt America, consumed by business, by money, by the restless urge to get ahead, no questions asked. "There is a widely accepted theory that crime does not pay. This may be true in many cases, but it was not always true in Chicago," noted the con man Joseph "Yellow Kid" Weil dryly. Milo Lewis was quite at home.

Photographs of Lewis show a fine-boned and almost feminine-looking young man with full lips, crinkly black hair, and dark, brilliant eyes. He was prepared to work hard, and he had something magnetic and determined about him. He took a job in the men's section of the big department store Marshall Field, selling suits and ties, but at night he put himself through the Chicago-Kent College of Law, and he quit Marshall Field when he was called to the Illinois State Bar in 1908. Having opened a small law office off Michigan Avenue, he was soon part owner of a couple of Chicago restaurants and a chain of newsstands. The lively Milo kept fingers in many pies. He enjoyed travel, fine food, expensive liquors, and especially the company of women. He was a man of great energy and fine, if predictable, tastes that he needed plenty of money to continue cultivating.

In 1909 he'd been in practice for little more than a year and was recently married, to Ethel Lewis, the daughter of a wealthy Chicago businessman. All was set fair when a friend introduced him to a prospective client—Sudie Whittaker, then in her thirties, a widow with two children, an attractive woman (as the *Des Moines Tribune* would describe her) with coils of dark hair and almond-shaped, almost oriental eyes.

Whittaker told Lewis she was involved with a business that had become so successful she needed a lawyer. She asked if he had heard of the great English admiral Sir Francis Drake, and Lewis replied that of course he had. Then she began to spin him her story about Drake's illegally probated estate. First she handed him a lengthy and impressive document, carefully typed, and sealed with wax and ribbon. It was entitled "Genealogical Report on the Claim to the Drake Estate" and had been prepared by a London genealogist named Rundle U. Upham, a name that might have occurred to Charles Dickens in one of his happier moments.

The document began:

First of all it is necessary to note a fact of vital importance to a clear understanding of the genealogy. In the days of Queen Elizabeth above all the other Drakes in Devon, two families were prominent, an old one and a new one, with apparently separate lineage and seated in opposite corners of the county of Devon. The old family Drake of Ash in the parish of Musbury on the Dorset border of East Devon, then represented by Sir Bernard Drake of Ash, and the new family of Drake of Buckland, then represented by its founder the celebrated Sir Francis Drake. Sir Bernard Drake of Ash, a gentleman of blue blood and coat armour, was knighted by Queen Elizabeth for his naval exploits and might have had a more enduring fame had his star not been eclipsed in the splendour of Sir Francis Drake whose rise from the mists of obscurity to the pinnacle of fame is a matter of history familiar to all.

Having established that there were two rival Drake families in Devon, and having therefore conveniently opened the door for all sorts of confusion, Upham (he did exist, and was a genealogist, though it's reasonable to assume that his deductions were tailored to Whittaker's no doubt specific requirements) plunged into the obscurities of Drake genealogy, tracing Sir Francis Drake's line down to the Rev. Bampfield (or Bamfield) Drake, rector of the parishes of Treborough in Somerset and Farway in Devon. Bampfield Drake was buried at Farway on June 20, 1729, and he left five sons. Upham noted:

> The two younger sons John and William died in England leaving issue. What became of the three elder sons has been a mystery. They just disappear leaving no record behind them. I have been able to prove all the male descendants of the first baronet except the three elder sons of the Rev. Bampfield Drake and these three brothers are in the line of entail for inheriting the estates.

Upham next investigated one possible and crucial reason for the disappearance of the three brothers from all British genealogical records. He referred to the "oft-recurring" tradition that the three brothers emigrated to America. He discussed the likelihood that "one was scalped by Indians while hunting with Daniel Boone in Kentucky and another fell in the War of the Revolution." He raised the issue of the unknown fate of the third brother and offered this advice: "Further investigation should be made to prove the tolerably clear assertion that some line of the American Drakes are the only true heirs to the Drake Estates and one of them is entitled to the baronetcy."

From Sudie Whittaker's point of view, here was the key selling point: Sir Francis Drake's true heir was an American.

Another piece of evidence she showed Milo Lewis on that day in 1909 wasn't so colorful. It was a letter written by George Nash, an

Indiana attorney. Nash, lacking the ornate turn of Rundle U. Upham, proceeded instead with a regular drumbeat of authority: "Said estate should have descended as aforesaid to Joseph Drake, then to his eldest son, Bampfield Drake, and to his son Joseph, upon whose male issue said estate has been entailed as aforesaid, then to Samuel Drake, then to his son Nathaniel, then to his son Joseph, and on in unbroken succession until George Drake is reached, who is the present owner and entitled to possession of said estate."

And so, Sudie Whittaker said, the heir was indeed an American, was, in fact, George Drake, who was alive and well and living in Roarchport, Missouri. And this George Drake, it so happened, was her cousin. But since her cousin George Drake was a man of only modest means and unable to carry the entire burden of pursuing the matter through the English courts, he had agreed to let some of his relatives in on the deal in exchange for their financial help; and, in turn, many of the relatives had granted Sudie Whittaker power of attorney to divide up their interests and sell shares, or subcontracts, as she called them.

This is how the Drake Estate scam, as peddled by Sudie Whittaker, was working in 1909. By then she was the most successful Drake promoter in America. She'd baffled both the authorities and her own investors for quite some time already. One of the clever things she did was never to reveal just how many relatives George Drake had; she kept adding to the list so that she could sell more subcontracts, then she would willfully alienate those investors she thought had been bled dry so they'd give up on their hopes and not bother her anymore. She sold the subcontracts, the shares, at $25 each.

Milo Lewis was intrigued, but not yet ready to bite. He told Sudie Whittaker he wanted to consider all the evidence. To do this he would have to go to England, he said, and he wanted her to pay for the trip. At the very least, he thought, he'd get a junket out of it.

Sudie Whittaker agreed, and Milo Lewis crossed to the other side of the Atlantic, where a variety of love affairs began: with Europe, with another woman, and with the financial possibilities of the Drake con. He traveled to Plymouth to inspect Buckland Abbey and the various other properties that had once been Sir Francis Drake's. Lawyers told him that the current head of the Drake family, the previously mentioned Lady Drake, had recently published a two-volume Drake genealogy, establishing her rights once and for all. Milo Lewis examined these volumes and realized that, far from being the authoritative obstacle that Lady Drake intended, the volumes could even be a tool. After all, why bother to publish unless Lady Drake was worried about litigation from those pesky American Drakes in Iowa and Ohio and elsewhere? The very existence of these books conjured up the possibility that she was merely trying to put investigators off the scent.

Lewis knew that he didn't have to believe in this scenario entirely; he only had to suggest that it could be the case. These were murky waters, and highly exploitable.

For this version of how Milo Lewis and Sudie Whittaker came to be working together I've relied on an account Lewis later gave to the Supreme Court of Illinois. It rings true (the court accepted it) as statement of fact which at no point asks us to enter into, or excuse, his state of mind. Lewis never let on whether he believed in the existence of the Drake Estate, or the chances of its being won for the American faction. As a lawyer he was inclined, indeed trained, to reserve judgment, and while no doubt skeptical about everything he'd heard from Sudie Whittaker, he satisfied himself that there was just enough meat and fact in the fantastic saga to make *disproving* it a very difficult job indeed. He was a lawyer, true, but a lawyer from Chicago, the city which had coined the business motto "Buy old junk cheap, fix it up a little, unload it on the other fellow," a formula that could be applied to all sorts of business deals and not only the Drake.

Lewis told Whittaker that he was in. For his services she rewarded him with a retainer, plus commission and expenses. Having positioned himself next to the revenues flowing to Whittaker from her investors, this clever and pushy man proceeded to expand his operations. He opened an office in Manhattan, a few city blocks south of Wall Street on Broadway, and in the next few years was a frequent visitor to London. In Chicago, when war broke out, he was invited to deliver a series of lectures about the European situation. It seemed by then that he was a man of the world: traveled, wealthy, learned, in control of himself and his life.

A part of Lewis's evolving performance was the keeping of a girl-friend or mistress in every city he visited. His wife, Ethel, soon tired of this and divorced him in the Superior Court of Cook County, Illinois, in November 1914. The grounds were desertion, and both the specific terms of the decree and the state laws of Illinois at that time prohibited Lewis from marrying anyone else within a year. This was to dog him.

Sudie Whittaker, meanwhile, went on doing what she did best, walking into rooms filled with strangers and persuading them to hand over their money. The slightness and slenderness of her physique belied a forceful character that mixed nerve, charm, and unwavering confidence. Traveling through Iowa, Kentucky, Indiana, and Missouri, even venturing as far afield as California, on arrival in a town she would check in to the best hotel and call a series of meetings, having let it be known through the local newspaper and the Chamber of Commerce that she had a business proposition.

At these meetings she pitched the story of the Drake Estate and of the subcontracts, or shares, that she was empowered to sell. Often she stayed several months in the same place, letting her good news spread, so that more and more suckers came forward, worried about missing out on the big deal. She offered a return of five hundred to one or even a thousand to one, making the Drake sound a lot like the sort of investment opportunity we saw in the late 1990s—one that sounds too good to be true but might on the other hand be too good to miss.

The way Sudie Whittaker worked seems remote to us now: the train journeys, the arrival in a town where one's business is unknown, the slowness of communication—these belong to another time, to the tail end of the frontier era. But the appeal of the dodge is perennial: Whittaker called to her suckers' optimism, to their naiveté and anxiety, to their restless and ever-present and energizing desire for wealth. Aided and advised by Milo Lewis, she worked her classic game without flaw and with increasing success; but then Oscar Hartzell came into her life, and although she would have her revenge on him in the end, Hartzell was her bad luck charm.

⌒

Milo Lewis always claimed that he and Whittaker gave Hartzell a job as a favor to Hartzell's mother, who had invested $6,500 in their scheme. Hartzell's telling was more dramatic, with a plum role for himself. He said that around Christmastime in 1914 he was summoned to a hotel in Monmouth, Illinois, because there was a crisis that called for his business acumen. A distant relative of his, together with "some man from Kansas," both big believers in the Drake Estate, had been alarmed by the outbreak of war in Europe and what this might mean for the prospects of getting their hands on the money; with this in mind they'd traveled to England to look into the matter, and had found that nobody over there seemed to have even heard of the Sir Francis Drake Estate. So now they'd come back home and were raising a stink. Was the scheme a hoax, a scam, a fraud, after all? How could Whittaker and Lewis explain themselves?

This was what the meeting in the Monmouth Hotel was about. Hartzell said that he walked into this situation, listened to all the different stories, and smoothed things over by pronouncing that the deal sounded fine. He called for drinks and raised a Christmas toast: "To this time next year—when we'll all be millionaires." Whittaker and Lewis were so impressed by his calm head and stern stand that they invited him to join their venture on the spot, he said.

Whichever of these different accounts, Oscar the humble employee or Oscar the businessman diplomatist, is true, by the beginning of 1915, Hartzell was working full-time for Sudie Whittaker and Milo Lewis. He traveled through Indiana, Illinois, the Dakotas, and Iowa, selling subcontracts in the Drake Estate. "I got very much enthused and interested in the matter," he said. He accepted payment from Whittaker and Lewis not in cash but in the form of shares, and I think we need no greater proof of his good faith at this point, at the beginning of his involvement with the scheme. In 1915 he believed in the basic proposition of the Drake Estate, accepted that a fortune was there for the taking if the people pursuing it were determined and clever enough. This didn't sound as farfetched to him then as it does to us now. After all, there really were cases of Americans becoming the sudden beneficiaries of wills left by distant relatives in the old country. And there were plenty of people called Drake throughout the Midwest, many of them descendants, through some obscure branch of the family but descendants nonetheless, of the great corsair himself. It was legend that in Cincinnati a doctor named Drake had once treated and saved Abraham Lincoln, although people didn't know then what he'd treated him for (it was syphilis). In Iowa there was a town called Drakeville.

For Hartzell, then, the scheme had a rough-and-ready plausibility, certainly enough to satisfy him when he was at rope's end. He put aside his years of expertise in farming and stock-raising and devoted himself to the Drake Estate. He became a disciple, a shift that signified a huge divide in his career and life.

⌒

In the summer of 1915, Sudie Whittaker was in Des Moines, Iowa, where she took a suite of rooms at the Hotel Chamberlain. As usual she alerted the local Chamber of Commerce and the local newspaper, in this case the *Des Moines Register*. A reporter who came to see her about the Drake Estate wrote: "Suddenly the hotel door opened and in walked a heavy-set, ruddy-complexioned man with a cigar between his teeth."

In walked Hartzell, who proceeded to berate Whittaker for talking to a newspaperman. Didn't she realize? If the public learned that the Drake treasure was about to be distributed it would have a simply terrible effect—the heirs would be pestered to death by people after the money.

This intrusion, so obviously scripted and staged, worked like magic. The reporter regretted that he could not suppress the story—and the resulting publicity was very good for business. A witness who attended one of her meetings remembered Sudie Whittaker coming back from lunch at around two in the afternoon to find twenty or thirty people waiting for her. According to this witness, she asked a man—presumably it was Hartzell—if the "class" was ready, and then, while the "class" sat in chintz-adorned chairs or on the windowsills smoking cigars, she told the story of the Drake Estate, with a couple of new twists specially devised for this Iowa crowd. She upped the ante a little, saying that an investment of $50 would bring a return of $100,000; and she introduced a note of urgency, revealing that the estate would be settled within weeks, since both the English courts and the English Parliament had just recognized the estate as belonging to George Drake and the other relatives whose power of attorney she had.

She was asked if she had any papers, any documentary evidence that this estate actually existed.

"I don't need that," Sudie Whittaker said. "Everybody takes my word for that."

Not just money would be theirs, she said. An entire city would fall into their hands! And she told them about Plymouth, a wealthy place of 150,000 inhabitants with a big wall around it, which would be a part of the settlement.

Possibly it was Sudie Whittaker who dazzled the Iowans, or Rundle U. Upham's genealogical evidence, or the reassuring presence of local boy Oscar Hartzell, or this idea of the ancient walled city of Plymouth; or maybe it was just the vision of Drake's *Golden Hind* riding low in the water, stuffed with the wealth of the Incas. In any event the good people of Des Moines plunged in droves. A judge of the circuit court, the county clerk, a justice of the peace, and various leading Des Moines society women were among those who invested. A farmer named Ralph Gorham and his mother mortgaged their farm and handed over $10,000. Sudie Whittaker collected $64,000 within a matter of weeks.

But then there was a hitch: on August 9, 1915, an unsporting gentleman named William Alstrand had her arraigned before the grand jury on charges of fraud; she'd sold him two shares for $50 on June 14, more than three weeks had passed, and he hadn't received his $100,000. Alstrand wanted his money, all of it, or for Sudie Whittaker to go to jail.

Milo Lewis was called to Des Moines. Acting on his advice, Whittaker pleaded not guilty, secured release on bail, and was summoned to appear back in court at the beginning of 1916. By then, however, she and Lewis had fled, braving the Kaiser's U-boats and the winter Atlantic storms to fetch up in wartime England.

Oscar Hartzell traveled with them from Iowa and thence on the risky voyage to Southampton. It was he who'd raised the money for the trip at short notice, persuading the hapless Ralph Gorham to hand over a further $8,000. Hartzell still looked like a farmer, still talked a rough farmer's language, and must have seemed incongruous entering the first-class lounges alongside the two slick promoters. If indeed he ever got that far—maybe Whittaker and Lewis bought him only a second- or third-class ticket, for they were under the impression that they were taking him along as an employee, little better than a servant; but this servant was vain and touchy and hot-tempered and harbored bigger dreams than either of them. He also had charm and an ability to inspire trust; in time he'd steal their scheme from under their noses.

The confidence man wasn't always called the confidence man. In America he was known first as "the diddler," after the swindling cheat in J. Kenney's now-forgotten play *Jeremy Diddler*. In his 1840 essay "Diddling, Considered as One of the Exact Sciences," Edgar Allan Poe analyzed the nature of this character's behavior. Diddling, Poe discovered, was a compound of "minuteness" (because the diddler's activities tend to be on a small scale—should he be tempted into big-time speculation he would lose his special character and become a *financier*), "interest" (your diddler always looks to number one and is guided only by self-interest), "perseverance" (he is not easily discouraged), "ingenuity" (he understands plot, he invents and circumvents—were he not a diddler he would be, say, a fisherman, or the inventor of patent traps for rats), "audacity" (he is bold, and conquers by will), "nonchalance" (he is cool and calm, never seduced into hurry or flurry), "originality" (his ideas are his own), "impertinence" (he swaggers, he sneers in your face as well as taking your money and even kicking your dog), and "grin" (his work done at night, he sets his head on his pillow and allows himself a smile at his own ingenuity and the gullibility of the world).

It must have seemed to Poe that "the diddler" was a term for the ages, but on July 7, 1848, William Thompson was arrested in New York, causing a sensation. The *New York Herald* reported:

ARREST OF THE CONFIDENCE MAN

For the last few months a man has been travelling the city, known as the "Confidence Man"; that is, he would go up to a perfect stranger in the street, and being a man of genteel appearance, would easily command an interview. Upon his interview he would say, after some little conversation, "have you confidence in me to trust me with your watch until tomorrow?"; the stranger, at this novel request, supposing him to be some old acquaintance, not at the moment recollected, allows him to take the watch, thus placing "confidence" in the honesty of the stranger, who walks off laughing, and the other, supposing it to be a joke, allows him to do so. In this way many have been duped.

This, as Johannes Dietrich Bergmann notes in his 1969 essay "The Original Confidence Man," is the earliest known use of the expression "confidence man." In an amusing and dramatic way, Thompson stripped a street hustle to its lean essentials: he made the sucker assume that the sucker could have confidence in him and then demanded that this confidence be demonstrated. But what else was going on here? From Thompson's point of view he was controlling the situation, projecting confidence—he wanted that watch, he was going to get it, and when he did he would enjoy a good laugh, a great big grin at his own cleverness and cheek and will and the sucker's stupidity. But what about the sucker? Why would anyone hand over his watch to a complete stranger? Because the stranger was behaving like a friend, like an intimate; perhaps the sucker wondered if he knew this fellow after all and had merely forgotten about him. The sucker's routine had been disrupted and he was, for a moment, shaken out of himself, and in this moment of vulnerability he was being called upon to live up to his own mask of goodwill and bonhomie and niceness. The confidence man punctured the shell of his own confidence and turned him into a softer version of himself.

Jeremy Diddler, Jonathan Wild, Moll Flanders, Richard Head, and countless other picaresque rogues both real and fictional had enacted similar dramas to fleece their victims down the ages, but Thompson earned the title "confidence man," obviously enough, because he used the word "confidence" in the script of his scam.

Three days later the *Herald* ran another piece, worth quoting at length:

> During the last week or ten days, the public have been entertained by the police reporters with several amusing descriptions of the transactions of a certain financial genius, who

rejoices in the soubriquet of the "Confidence Man." It appears that the personage who has earned this euphonious and winning description, has been in the habit of exercising his powers of moral suasion to an extent attained by the very greatest of our temperance preachers. Accosting a well-dressed gentleman in the street, the "Confidence Man," in a familiar manner, and with an easy nonchalance, would playfully put the enquiry—"Are you really disposed to put any confidence in me?" This interrogatory, thus put, generally met an affirmative answer. After all, there is a great deal of the milk of human kindness even in the inhabitants of great cities, and he must be a very obdurate sinner who can resist a really scientific appeal to his vanity. "Well, then," continues the "Confidence Man," "just lend me your watch until tomorrow!" The victim, already in the snare of the fowler, complies, with a grin; and the "Confidence Man" disappears around the next corner. Tomorrow comes, but not with it the watch, or the charmer; and Mr. "Done Brown" finally awakes to a sense of his folly, when he tells his sad story, amid the suppressed titterings of hardhearted policemen, in the office of Mr. Justice McGrath, at the Tombs. Fate, however, is hard. It may be true that fortune favors the brave; but sometimes, with malicious joy, she puts the bravest in limbo. The "Confidence Man," at present, occupies a very small apartment in a famous building in Center Street.

The writer, having aired his glee at the discovery of this character, goes on to make another connection:

As you saunter through some of the fashionable streets and squares which ornament the upper part of this magnificent city, you cannot fail to be struck by the splendor of some of the *palazzos* which meet the eye in all directions. Lordly dwellings are they, of marble and granite—with imposing porticoes—and great windows of stained glass—and extensive conservatories filled with rarest exotics—and massive doors and stairways of costly wood—and curiously carved with gilded balustrades—and lofty ceilings, painted in the highest style of modern ornamental art—and superb chandeliers—and grand dressoirs, loaded with vessels of gold and silver—and luxurious coaches covered with the richest velvet—and tapestried carpets yielding like a mossy bank beneath the foot—and beds of softest down, with coverings of tapestry, with carved works, with fine linen of Egypt, and perfumed with myrrh, aloes and cinnamon! Splendid equipages, with coachmen and footmen, and valets and attendants of all sorts, arrayed in livery, very flaming and *outré* to be sure, are waiting in front of those places for their precious freight, composed of the snub-nosed matrons and daughters of those aristocratic houses. Over the whole scene there is an air of that ostentatious expenditure, and that vulgar display in which the possessors of suddenly acquired wealth are so prone to gratify their low and selfish feelings. But still there are all the evidences of a lavish and most profligate expenditure. Our curiosity is excited. We exclaim:—

> "The things you see are vastly rich and rare,
> We wonder how the devil they got there!"

After all, the mystery may be readily resolved. Those *palazzos*, with all their costly furniture, and all their splendid equipages, have been the product of the same genius in their proprietors, which has made the "Confidence Man" immortal and a prisoner at the Tombs. His genius has been employed on a small scale in Broadway. Theirs has been employed in Wall

Street. That's all the difference. He has obtained half a dozen watches. They have pocketed millions of dollars. He is a swindler. They are exemplars of honesty. He is a rogue. They are financiers. He is collared by the police. They are cherished by society. He eats the fare of a prison. They enjoy the luxuries of a palace. He is a mean, beggarly, timid, narrow-minded wretch who has not a *sou* above a chronometer. They are respectable, princely, bold, high-soaring "operators" who are to be satisfied only with the plunder of a whole community.

The unnamed writer's identification with "the confidence man" is so instantaneous as to suggest that something more than reporting is going on. A key myth has been given a name. The confidence man is a crook, but he is ingenious. The sheer brazen bravado and disarming cheek of his crime raise a smile, both at his audacity and the gullibility of his victim. Moreover, the confidence man's particular way of thumbing his nose at the law also reveals something about the workings of money and power. Many big businessmen are no better than he, but they get away with their crimes, his only mistake being that he doesn't operate on a grand enough scale and can't afford to keep a judge or two in his pocket.

A sympathetic nerve had been touched, and this new usage, "confidence man," passed so quickly into everyday currency that only eight years later, on April Fool's Day 1857, Herman Melville (whose own father had been driven into bankruptcy and madness by a shady business deal) published a novel, his last, entitled *The Confidence Man*, about a morphing riverboat swindler on the Mississippi. *The Confidence Man* baffled Melville's contemporaries and pretty much finished off his literary career. Now the book reads like an extraordinarily prescient examination of the yeasty relationship between American optimism, American greed, and American deceit.

All the people in Melville's story are money-driven, money-mad, an obsession that reveals their true nature to the confidence man and leaves them open to his schemes. These include the setting up of "The World's Charity," the running of "the Seminole Asylum," and the selling of shares in the "Black Rapids Coal Company." The splendid and sinister name of this last venture suggests that Melville's hero might be an agent of the devil, might even be Beelzebub himself. Like other satanic representatives before and since, he plays the part of instructor, exposing the wise man's folly. Out of the confidence man's deceit comes truth—about greed, about the dangers of believing in the basic goodness of man and nature, about the way people are once their masks are dropped. His fooling is cruel indeed, because he fools people with their hopes. He calls upon his victims' fantasy and fear that the bigger thing, the better thing, the real thing is happening somewhere else, but—guess what?—they can have it too. All they have to do is dare, believe, show no fear. Then he leaves them hanging, voided. It's the story of the American swindle from the snake-oil salesman to the Internet chat-room huckster. As Yellow Kid Weil once remarked to Saul Bellow: "They wanted something for nothing. I gave them nothing for something."

⁓

There were five in the party: there was Milo Lewis, now married to his second wife, Nettie, the young Englishwoman he'd met on the earlier trip to London; there was Sudie Whittaker, who brought along her twelve-year-old son; and there was Hartzell, whose first British immigration card carried a sepia-toned photograph showing a personable and well-groomed man of early middle age, mild and seemingly harmless in appearance, the sort of fellow who looked as though he would be anxious to please anybody. The address Hartzell gave to customs and the police was ℅ the *Chicago Daily News*, London, a suitably vague address for the blank of a whole new life that was beginning. The Americans arrived in Southampton on January 3, 1916, and at once took the train to London, where they put up in the smart and pricey Park Lane Hotel.

Barrage balloons floated high in the skies, gleaming silver at night when the city was blacked out for fear of attack by German zeppelins. Soldiers hurried through the railway stations, on their way to France, or coming back for leave or on stretchers. England had already lost 250,000 men and the disaster of the Somme (more than 60,000 men on a single day) was only six months away. Ambulances honked and chuttered in the muddy streets and posters demanded from every wall: "WHAT DID YOU DO IN THE GREAT WAR, DADDY?"; "WHAT WILL YOUR BEST GIRL SAY IF YOU'RE NOT IN KHAKI?" A certain proportion of the British populace thought it was at war to save not only the Empire but civilization itself, and the Americans, the bloody Yanks, weren't quite trusted because they hadn't yet joined the good fight against the Kaiser.

Whittaker, Lewis, and Hartzell plunged oblivious into this heady atmosphere of jingoism. Escaping to the chaos of the Old World from the encroaching law of the New, set on a convoluted scheme of fiscal gain, they gave no indication of caring a damn about the war or about anything except vying for control of their criminal enterprise. It was a story that Henry James would have relished: Americans abroad pursuing their own plot of greed and betrayal.

Lewis had saved Sudie Whittaker in Des Moines and now exacted his price, demanding that he become the leader, the figurehead, of the Drake scheme, and that, more significant, all revenues flow directly to him. Their situations were to be exactly reversed:

she would get a small salary, plus expenses and commission, as he had before. And he wanted her with him in London so he could keep an eye on her.

Whittaker unhappily agreed to this flip-flop of power but wasn't about to settle for it. She was constantly going behind Lewis's back, trying to arrange with her people back home that the Drake money should still be sent to her. Hartzell's job was to stay close by her side and make sure that if any money did come it went at once to Lewis. So when, after a few weeks at the Park Lane Hotel, the Americans moved into rented apartments, Lewis ordered Hartzell to live with Whittaker and her son. Unsurprisingly, this led to friction and argument.

Was there anything sexual between Whittaker and Hartzell? Did she try to seduce him to her side?

In 1936, in prison writing his autobiography, Hartzell recalled an episode from much earlier in his life. He'd apparently staked a friend of his, a prospector, and let him have $500 to go look for gold in Colorado. About a year and a half later, Hartzell's story went, the friend summoned him to collect his share.

Hartzell wrote:

> He had struck some gold and had between 12 & 13 thousand dollars panned out. Half was mine. I stayed with him about a week. It took me two days to ride the 60 miles each way and coming back I brought my half of the gold and his also to put in the bank for him. He told me to take a different road back because he'd heard there was a halfway house where I could stop the night. I put my pony in the barn and went to the house, it was a large log house, a sort of hotel.
>
> I found a woman there, very good looking. I got my supper and she showed me to a room upstairs but there was no-

one else about that I could see or hear and I said to her, "Do you live up here in the wild all alone?" and she said she did but things did not seem right to me. I had a hunch that trouble was ahead for me because I had all that gold.

I was not in a hurry about taking off my clothes but I was very tired riding all day down the mountain. I took off my ducking coat, my coat, my waistcoat, and my six shooters and hung them on the hook on the door. I had not taken off my western hat and my high boots when there was a rap at the door. It was the woman and she wanted to know if everything was alright. I told her it was and she started to try to be fresh and put her arms around me. She seemed to want to keep her arms over my ears so I said, "The door's not locked, I'd better lock it," and as I went to lock the door I let the key fall on the floor on purpose. The bed was extra high and had curtains on the side of the bed but the curtains didn't fit too close and I saw a man under the bed.

I reached for my six shooters and I jumped right on top of the bed and told her to get down on the floor on her hands and knees p.d.q. She did and then I told the man to crawl out from under the bed or I would shoot him through the mattress. I told him to crawl out on his hands and knees with no gun in his hand or I would drill them both. I made them crawl down the stairs. I got my coats that had the gold in and kept one gun on them while I back out the door and went to the log barn and got my pony and went about two miles in the wood along the ravine and slept under the trees with my gold and ducking coat for a pillow but I did not sleep but little.

That was one of the closest calls I ever had. If I had not discovered him first no-one knows what may have happened. I did not want to kill them unless I had to but I would have

drilled them both for I knew it was them or me in a place like
that. All my life after that I always take a peek under the bed
no difference where I am.

Dr. Clark Mangun, the psychiatrist who encouraged Hartzell to
put down on paper a record of his life, said that this hilarious and
quite fantastic episode was just that, a fantasy. "It would make good
fiction," he noted. There's no suggestion anywhere else in all the
various records that Hartzell staked a prospector or ever went to
Colorado; nor was he adept at gunplay. But this was an imaginative
stroke from a man whose flights into fancy were always telling.
Hartzell liked to think of himself as practical and hard-nosed, a businessman whose only interest was cash, the bottom line. Ideas of
wealth and success affected him like an opiate, however, and even if
the story was indeed a fairy tale, something out of the Brothers
Grimm festooned with the trappings of the Western dime novel, its
driving force was the vision of himself as a frontiersman, hell bent
on making it, and fighting for his stake against all odds. There's interest too in the emotional scenario within the fantasy: the pot of gold,
the temptress, the sneaky would-be thief, the closeness of a danger
that was defeated only by the attitude and bold decisiveness of the
pioneer hero.

This story was a blueprint of how he saw his relationship with
Whittaker and Lewis, and in constructing this section of his autobiography I think he was writing in a veiled way of how he van-
quished his adversaries, and of the pride this made him feel.
Interestingly, as we'll see later, he never allowed himself to write
about this directly; what happened "on the other side of the water"
was always to be kept secret from the American authorities. But he
did admit that confusion, anxiety, and uncertainty made those early
years and months in London the worst time of his life. Even his

resolutely upbeat salesman's personality was beaten down. He was impoverished and far from home. He was in a strange country that he hadn't come to know yet, and he was surrounded by people he didn't like and on whom he needed to rely. He probably wondered from time to time what the hell he was doing. And Sudie Whittaker didn't encourage him or take him as a lover. Probably she would have found such an idea ridiculous. Instead she bossed him about and made him run errands. Doubtless he was humiliated. Yet out of this came what he reckoned his greatest triumph and success. He was six-gun Oscar, his pistols loaded with stratagems not bullets, the con-man underdog who in time made his superiors crawl. What he lacked in subtlety he made up for in nerveless and almost terrifying will. He was writing about London, not Colorado, when he said:

"It was them or me in a place like that."

In 1916, Milo Lewis was still in charge, and, although expansive and extravagant and even reckless, Lewis was never smug. He knew a threat to his control might come, but didn't see that Hartzell could be its source. Sudie Whittaker was the problem, and the authorities back in America. He had Whittaker followed all over town and busied himself preparing a lawsuit that he filed in the English Court of Chancery in 1917. The Missouri man George Drake had died a few months before, so Lewis lodged the claim on behalf of George's son, Ernest. The lawsuit's gist was this: that Ernest Drake was rightfully entitled to the Drake baronetcy, and should henceforth be known as Sir Ernest Drake.

It was very clever on Milo Lewis's part, for if Drake's fortune did indeed exist as a legal entity, and if claim were to be made to it on Ernest Drake's behalf, then a demand for the baronetcy was a necessary legal preliminary. The tactic showed Whittaker's people back home that he'd now taken complete command and was hurrying things along. Most important, he had now created, at the expense of a few pounds and a couple of hours of his time, a document he could point to and say, "I had good intent." He was covering himself.

Hartzell, caught between these two seemingly cleverer compatriots, wrote letters back home in which he inflated his role, assuring his friends and relatives that he'd checked everything out and satisfied himself that the fortune was for real. Milo Lewis and he had toured London, he said, eyeing many of the important buildings that were tied up in the settlement. In fact, Lewis kept Hartzell in the dark and on a short leash, throwing him a few pounds each week and the occasional gift of clothes. At this point Hartzell had little idea what was going on; he was, in the parlance of the con, "on the outside."

He'd decided not to bring his wife, Daisy, with him to England. Years later he told a prison psychiatrist that there was no extra money for the ticket. More likely, he'd given up on the marriage. For a while he and Daisy wrote letters to and fro, but she began to press him about when the estate would be settled and when he was coming home, whereupon he ceased the correspondence. By the middle of 1917, America was in the war, and it was suddenly fun again to be an American in London. He'd found himself a string of girlfriends and saw each of them every week or so, sometimes sleeping with them, always using (as he put it) "a conundrum," i.e., a condom.

One of his girlfriends was Eunice Colliss, the twenty-two-year-old daughter of the manager at Bewlay's, an upscale tobacco store on the Strand where he bought his cigars. He sold himself to her as a successful American businessman, in England to pursue a fortune to add to the one he had already. The flower of English youth was on the other side of the Channel, so Eunice's door was open for Oscar. She took tea with her rugged Midwestern beau, walked with him along Piccadilly, sat side by side with him in the motion picture palaces and through vaudeville shows. Soon they were weekending together, at her parents' small house by the sea, in Hove, near Brighton. Hartzell didn't use his conundrums quite diligently enough, for on April 12, 1918, Eunice gave birth to a son, christened Wilson Hartzell Colliss. Hartzell promised her that as soon as his divorce came through he'd marry her and they'd get a house together. He even borrowed £500 from her father to set them on their way.

Hartzell did get his divorce—or rather, Daisy got hers, granted on grounds of desertion, at the beginning of 1919—but he didn't marry Eunice. By then there had been so many fights with Sudie Whittaker that Lewis let him off the hook and agreed to his finding a place of his own. Hartzell answered an ad in the *Times* and rode the Underground out to Ealing, in West London, where on a quiet suburban street, in a red brick suburban three-story house, he encountered a woman who was in many ways Sudie's English equivalent, although for more than a decade she would be on his side, his future landlady and mentor-to-be, a widow in her thirties named Mrs. E. A. Broadburn. On seeing her face lit with a smile, Hartzell had a winning moment and said he'd call her Joy. He stuck with the name always thereafter, although what began as a romance would be complicated by money, money.

At first Hartzell told Joy Broadburn that he was an American businessman, on close terms with Montagu Norman, the head of the Bank of England. Writing in 1933, she took up the story of what happened:

He became a boarder in my home in 1919 & with the usual nonsense, promises galore, became non-paying, telling me that he was in England with a crowd to establish the "Drake" heirs. I told him I was the adopted daughter of the only remaining Drake and foolishly gave into his hand the will that had been made in my favour. I never got back that, or any other thing that he took a fancy to and I let him take out of my house under the impression that this was a big thing and I should get it all back together! Then came the great day when he was received by the King and he asked me to let him have as a loan my Papa's ring, a pigeon blood ruby, his watch, seal, and fob, and mother's diamond horse-shoe broach which had 34 diamonds in it, all of which I valued very dearly and none of which I ever saw again, beside various loans of 250 pounds at a time.

All this poured out in a letter to Harry Reed, Hartzell's Sioux City prosecutor, when Joy Broadburn was looking to get back at least her ruby ring. The entire story of her thirteen-year relationship with Hartzell is compressed into one bitter paragraph. When this letter was read in court, Hartzell stood up and exclaimed: "The lady is a con woman." That moment was rich in irony, but it does seem that Joy Broadburn protested too much. Hartzell may well have made off with her jewels and family heirlooms, but it's not easy to swallow the sentence that goes, "I told him I was the adopted daughter of the only remaining Drake and foolishly gave into his hand the will that had been made in my favour." To believe that is to accept that Hartzell answered an advertisement and encountered a woman who not only had known Drake's last living relative but happened to have a will lying handy to prove it.

What really happened is that some time after Hartzell moved into Joy Broadburn's house the two of them became lovers. Part of the pillow talk involved the Drake Estate, and together they began to plot and plan. By now, Hartzell had seen enough of Whittaker and Lewis to know that they were crooks and the whole enterprise was a fraud. He'd witnessed them at work, fabricating the stage props of the con, such as fake family Bibles, forged parchments, messages that were carved on church pews, and a tombstone that had been made and inscribed in secret so it could be smuggled into a Plymouth graveyard at dead of night and photographed the next day as apparent confirmation of Ernest Drake's claim. But rather than turning Whittaker and Lewis in, or telling the people back home that they'd better not send any more money, he had another idea. He'd seen Lewis grab control from Whittaker, and now it would be his turn.

⌣

Hartzell hated Whittaker and Lewis with the venom of the powerless, but this didn't make vaulting over their interests any easier. He bided his time, content to let them think him a clumsy farmer, and he obligingly ran their errands, having Lewis's suits cleaned, or going with Whittaker's son to the zoo and to Charlie Chaplin movies or the theaters around Piccadilly Circus and Leicester Square. "It takes a clever man to play the idiot and do it properly," he told a friend. In thinking of himself as acting a role (Hartzell in Hamlet mode), he felt happier.

In April 1919 the Supreme Court of Illinois moved to disbar Milo Lewis, to strike him from its list of qualified and approved attorneys and strip him of the right to practice law. There were two counts: first, that he was fraudulently inducing people to invest in the bogus estate of Sir Francis Drake; second, that he'd committed perjury and bigamy in the state of Illinois, having married his second wife, Nettie, before his divorce from his first wife, Edith, had been made absolute.

This startling development began to propel the Drake swindle into its next phase.

Milo Lewis had indeed been reckless, and someone had informed on him. There were plenty of suspects. Both Whittaker and Hartzell wanted him out of the way, although they stood only to lose were the myth of the Drake Estate exploded. That rules them out. Presumably Edith Lewis wished her ex-husband little good, although the most likely candidate was Nettie herself, for by 1919 the footloose Lewis had branded her an adulteress, caused their marriage to be annulled in a court in New York, and was refusing to pay maintenance for their three-year-old child. Nettie Lewis, wronged and justifiably enraged, cried for revenge.

Lewis hurried back from London to answer the charges, and Whittaker and Hartzell both traveled with him to Chicago. Hartzell was once again given the salesman's job and sent out on the road to assure the investors that, despite this hiccup, all was well. Meanwhile Lewis prepared his defense, and was successful, arguing that he'd believed his marriage to Nettie legal and valid because it had taken place not in Illinois but in London, where different matrimonial rules applied. When it was pointed out that he'd lied to Nettie, telling her that his first marriage was over and done, he turned the tables by attacking her reputation, saying she was a woman of dubious virtue who'd taken advantage of him and was by no means to be believed. On the issue of the Drake Estate, the attorneys of the Illinois State Bar produced little in the way of concrete evidence, asking the court to accept that the scheme was *prima facie* preposterous. Lewis argued that as legal argument this wouldn't do, that no case had been presented for him to answer, and the court accepted his stance. His opponents had failed to prove that the Drake Estate did *not* exist—that is, they'd failed to prove a negative, a problem that was to haunt investigators and prosecutors for the next seventeen years. Lewis escaped.

Three years later, however, in June 1922, he was back in front of the court, and this time there'd been a thorough and detailed investigation. With regard to the Drake Estate, the court persisted in its belief: "On its face the venture appears to be a chase after a phantom, but who and where is the lawyer who has not at some time discovered to his sorrow that the case on which he had built high hopes of reward proved to be a shadow?"

Less indulgence was shown the baffling complexity of his matrimonial arrangements. This time Nettie Lewis's story was examined with more sympathy and in greater detail, and it emerged that within a few weeks of the annulment of her marriage to Lewis he'd married yet again, for the third time, to a Miss Draper, of Crown Point, Indiana. By 1922 this third marriage was on the rocks also. The court said: "When he was admitted to the Bar he took an oath to uphold the law, and it was his duty to do so and not to evade it or take advantage of any lack of uniformity in the divorce laws of this and other countries to accomplish that which the law of his state plainly prohibited. He seemed more concerned in keeping himself much married than in keeping within the law."

Lewis was disbarred, and Hartzell got the weapon he needed. The judgment allowed two conclusions: that Lewis was certainly a scoundrel, and that the Drake Estate only *might* be a phantom—but on the other hand might not. Thus the Supreme Court of Illinois, no less, gave permission to proceed as though the Drake scheme were on the up and up while simultaneously ripping away the mask of professional qualification and respectability that Milo Lewis had used to run and control the show. For Oscar the result couldn't have been more perfect.

I discovered the story of Milo Lewis's disbarment by following a lead from one of the psychiatric interviews conducted with Hartzell in 1936. During this interview, in the course of which Hartzell said a lot of crazy things, he referred to Lewis as "a disbarred lawyer." I thought this had to be worth looking into, so I contacted the Illinois State Bar and learned that Lewis had indeed been struck off its list in 1922. Next I got in touch with the Illinois Supreme Court itself to see if, by any chance, the records of these proceedings were still in existence. A few days later I heard from Juleann Hornyack, the clerk of the Supreme Court of Illinois, who told me, "I was up half the night reading this stuff. It's a fascinating story."

This was one of many lucky breaks that occurred during my research, for the batch of documents that Hornyack sent me revealed parts of the Hartzell story that had never been told before and provided context for much more. Here, for instance, were copies of Rundle U. Upham's genealogy, and the letter George Nash had written to Sudie Whittaker. Here was Milo Lewis's testimony, explaining how he had met Whittaker and how, exactly, the Drake scheme ran under her command. Here, most important, was the background for and beginnings of what became an increasingly frantic struggle for control of the con.

The next development in the story unfolded in a series of letters that Hartzell wrote over the next two years. Taken by themselves, these letters are opaque and not so easy to understand; read in the context of Lewis's disbarment, they vividly illustrate how Hartzell seized his chance and made the most of it.

Most of this correspondence is on notepaper from the London offices of the *Chicago Daily News*, where Hartzell plied his pen in the Visitors' Room, overlooking Trafalgar Square and Nelson's Column.

The letters were addressed to his supporters in Des Moines, with in-structions that they be read in secret and then forwarded to his mother in Monmouth for safekeeping. His handwriting was at times so excited as to be scarcely legible; it sloped sharply to the right and crammed the page, as if by covering even the tiniest fragments of white space with black ink he could also obliterate any doubt from his readers' minds. Every word of these letters burned with his rage and longing for control.

He stressed that a fortune, a once-in-a-life opportunity, was at stake. First he devoted himself to flat-out attacks on Whittaker and Lewis:

"Remember, I have been running with a very bad crowd. Being English yourself, you must know better than anyone that you have to have clean hands to gain success in the courts of England," he wrote to John Owen, an English émigré, an insurance adjuster in Des Moines. "An automobile couldn't haul the criminal records connected with that outfit. In 1916, in Plymouth, Lewis got a black-smith to do some dirty work. The next thing he did was to get the blacksmith's daughter into trouble. And you will not believe this be-cause it does not look believable but there is another woman that has six children by him. Hell's just a poppin! The records in the end will show a *score* of illegitimate children that belong to Lewis. All the money that you possess would not pay the damage that has been brought upon me by traveling with that bunch of crooks."

You will not believe this because it does not look believable. The nub of the con man's skill is to make you believe it anyway.

Hartzell started from the reasonable assumption that the Mid-western investors would probably be very angry indeed to learn that thousands of their hard-won dollars had merely bankrolled Milo Lewis's sexual misadventures. "They will go to jail for the rest of their lives when the crash comes for they have not been square with the people," he wrote, laying it on thick, accusing Whittaker and Lewis of perjury, forgery, bribery, and fraud.

It wasn't enough only to heap scorn on "those crookedest crooks" Whittaker and Lewis, though no doubt Hartzell gained immense satisfaction from so doing. He had determined not to hijack the con, as Lewis had done, but to reinvent it. So he had to be creative, and persuade his American audience to hold on to the vision of those coffers filled with gold and treasure, even if they were to be seen now from a different perspective that he said he would tell them about later, when everything was safe.

He introduced his own version of the scheme cleverly and piece by piece. Or was he improvising as he went along, feeling his way? His next step was to break the distressing news that all monies spent thus far had been squandered, not only because Lewis had used them to finance his various dalliances, but because the genealogy that Sudie Whittaker had relied on was all wrong. There'd never been any chance of their getting the fortune, he said, because George Drake wasn't the heir, and so Ernest Drake couldn't be either. Thus all the subcontracts that had been sold were worthless, and Whittaker and Lewis had known this since 1916.

"Go from the bottom. If Ernest Drake is not the heir—I will know who is," he wrote.

Meanwhile he asked his Des Moines allies to pass the word that all the Drake investors had better look matters square in the face. They'd lost everything they'd put in and could only conclude that Whittaker and Lewis were not competent to handle this delicate affair. He even predicted how Milo Lewis would react: "He will try coming to the States, and do as usual, and call you people to Chicago and let you stand around for hours and come down and appear to be mad and say that you all interfered with his work. He will say or do anything to excuse his damned criminal nonsense and get you to spend another $175,000."

A side effect of this tricky dance was the calling into being of the front that Hartzell would from then on always have ready for the folks back home. He was Honest Oscar, the straight shooter, maybe not that smart, maybe a plodder compared to the slick and suave Milo Lewis, but prepared to go to any lengths to do this right. He had hired all-new teams of lawyers and genealogists. He was using "legal talent whose standing and reputation and character are spotless and they are going over the ground from Sir Francis Drake's death, quietly, neatly, and tactfully."

Hartzell reeled in his suckers stridently, obsessively, cleverly. He would always be "square with the people," he said.

He also laid down another important part of his strategy, beginning to make a fetish of secrecy. "If I were starving and you were here with $5000 I should not tell you who my legal talent is," he wrote to the insurance adjuster Owen. "Matters are handled so diplomatically and cleverly and I will make no mistakes alone. You being from England, Mr. Owen, should know that it's all a question of wheels within wheels and wheels within those wheels and the inside wheels are the ones that succeed."

He said: "Just remember that O. M. Hartzell is top dog."

For a while the American Drakers didn't know where to turn or whom to believe. In the confusion a Milo Lewis man knocked at the door of one of Hartzell's people in Des Moines and threw a bucket of cold water in her face. Hartzell's advice to the woman was to have a lawyer on hand the next time Lewis's ally showed up and give him and any of his associates "a good suing."

Lewis, who saw an easy livelihood vanishing in front of his eyes, fought back against this criminal *coup d'état*. In those days the

American Express offices on London's Haymarket served as a club. Expatriates went there to drink coffee in the lounge or study the American newspapers in the reading room and not only to do their banking and collect their mail. It had been a routine of Lewis and Hartzell's business relationship in earlier days that they would meet there to catch up. They met there again on January 15, 1923. In fact they literally bumped into each other, just in front of the revolving doors. Appropriately, Hartzell was coming in, Lewis going out. It was the first time they'd seen each other in nine months, and Hartzell has left us a record of this Homeric encounter. He wrote in a letter:

"The brainstorm and noise of mouth started. I put myself into action and, believe me, I put the fear of God into that criminal skunk. He ran back into the American Express so he could have witnesses."

But the man who would be top dog was on the rampage and not to be put off. He didn't care even about the witnesses.

"I went in and gave him the graveyard look and rubbed my fist under his nose and told him he was a criminal and an embezzler, a disbarred lawyer and a forger, and a crooked skunk. The only thing that kept me from knocking him clear through the door is the law over here, but he would have got it anyway if he hadn't backed off."

Just as everything seemed to be swinging Hartzell's way, there was a hitch. He'd written to an Iowa friend, Dr. John Nixon, telling him that the Roarchport Drakes weren't the heirs and he would be commissioning a new genealogy to find out who the heir really was. Sudie Whittaker was back in America at that time and Nixon handed her the letter.

"I trusted Dr. Nixon like a father. He flatly betrayed me. Mrs. Whittaker came to London and brought a man by the name of Judge

Graves with her," Hartzell wrote in his autobiography, introducing this man Graves in tones appropriate to a villain from a spaghetti western. "He walked with a stoop, and wore a black hat, and was always smiling, a terrible smile. He was as big as a mountain, one *hell* of a looking piece of timber."

Sudie Whittaker had at once understood the danger Hartzell now presented: she could always hope to regain control of her end of things from Milo Lewis, but not if an entirely new version of the scheme had usurped her own. She and Lewis brought suit against Hartzell for writing the libelous letter to Nixon and for threatening and slandering Milo Lewis. The papers were served at American Express.

"They thought they had my grave all dug for me," Hartzell said.

But Whittaker, Lewis, and their legal adviser Judge Graves had made a miscalculation: Hartzell, the hayseed, knew his way around a courtroom. "He enjoyed being in court and was good at it," Daisy Hartzell said later. "It was like theater for him, and he was the leading player." All those years of lawsuits in Iowa now paid their dividend. He arrived in court with a topflight London barrister, a certified copy of Lewis's disbarral proceedings, newspaper clippings concerning Sudie Whittaker's grand jury indictment of 1915, and various of the phony Drake share certificates they'd sold him.

Hartzell wrote in a letter: "When Lewis's barrister saw all this staring him in the face all you could hear or my lawyers could hear was 'Ba-ba-ba, stop-stop-stop.' I made him the big billy goat and he got his whiskers pulled out by the roots, his arm knocked off, and his whole rear end tore off him."

In Hartzell's spelling, "legal" became "legle" and "whole" was "hole." He called this his cattle pasture language, but he knew what he was doing.

"It was murder in the first degree but I just took a light shot. Think what will happen when the heavy artillery starts barking. He got to see his own skeleton and it scared him to death."

Whittaker and Lewis lost their case, and were ordered to pay costs. The ominous Judge Graves beat his way back across the Atlantic, to feature only once more in this story. A few days later, Hartzell and Milo Lewis bumped into each other again, in the middle of Piccadilly Circus.

This time there was no face-off. "The minute he saw me he went the other way like a shot. He is finished," Hartzell wrote with superb contempt.

Here was the decisive moment. He'd won; he could take over.

THREE

Oscar, Master of Misrule

A round the time I became interested in Oscar Hartzell, more than three years ago, there was a story in the San Fernando Valley edition of the *Los Angeles Times*. A wealthy young businessman named Chris Rawlings had been carjacked at gunpoint and made to lie down in the trunk of his Bentley; there was a high-speed chase on the Hollywood Freeway, and in the ensuing crash, Rawlings was hurled from the Bentley's trunk. He died from his injuries.

The photograph accompanying this tragic story showed a boyish, fresh-faced, handsome young man, a loving husband and father by all accounts, an American winner smashed by malign fate while on the way to the convenience store. He'd been about to buy diapers for his baby girl.

This struck a nerve with me, because I have small children of my own and because Rawlings seemed to have been such a personable young man, with everything going for him. His friends spoke of his warmth, his charm, his ability to make anybody, even the kid washing his car, feel like a king. I tried to imagine how Rawlings's wife must feel, and reminded myself that this was part of what Los Angeles was and why you had to be careful here; but then, during the following days, there were other stories, stories revealing that, completely unknown to his family and friends, Chris Rawlings had been a big-time con artist, running a multitude of scams out of a telephone sales boiler room in a rented office on Wilshire Boulevard. He'd had a secret and illicit business life—selling shares in companies that didn't exist, luring backers for movies that would never be made.

One of Chris Rawlings's swindles had involved a claim to have discovered various long-lost recordings made by the soul singer Marvin Gaye. These were currently locked in a bank vault because of a probate dispute, he'd said, and what he needed, he'd told his investors, was a sum to help cover his legal expenses while he untangled the mess surrounding Gaye's will, in return for which he was prepared to sell points in the CD that would be released once all the issues were resolved. "Look how well those Beatles CDs have been doing. This is going to go like gangbusters," he'd told his suckers, who had no idea he was merely playing a riff on the Drake scheme.

It's very probable that Rawlings himself had never heard of Oscar Hartzell, but he knew he was putting a new twist on an old dodge, and his selection of contemporary detail was spot on: not the lost Bach cello recordings of Yo-Yo Ma (no one would have believed that, or even been interested probably), not the secret early demo tapes of Britney Spears (didn't somebody sell those already?), but Marvin Gaye, who had been murdered by his own father, and whose life had ended in the sort of controversy and mess that does indeed result in lawsuits and valuable material being locked away for years. Yes, people had thought, Marvin Gaye—there really could be something in that.

What the con man does is simple, and it's always the same. He presents the unreal as though it were truth. He does so in full knowledge that the particular part of the unreal he's talking about is *not* truth—but it makes an enchanting story. Usually he's *selling* something. It could be something that isn't his. In the early 1920s, around the time Hartzell was taking over in London, the Czech con man Victor Lustig contrived to sell the Eiffel Tower not once but twice, telling his suckers that the structure was rusting and needed expensive maintenance work, so the French government, rather than funding the repairs, had licensed him to get rid of the thing for scrap. Or it could be something that isn't what he says it is—like the fake Vermeer that the Dutch forger Hans van Meegeren sold to Hermann Göring, or the bogus Howard Hughes autobiography that McGraw-Hill bought from Clifford Irving, or, in the crudest version of this, a gold brick not made of gold. Or it could be something that isn't there or doesn't exist. The Drake Estate scheme itself is just an elaboration of a street hustle like the shell game or find-the-lady or three-card monte. These simple formulas are played out with an infinite number of variations, some necessarily blunt and direct, others very indirect and fantastically theatrical; and the variations themselves mutate over time, adapted by the clever con man to contemporary life and changes in the social atmosphere.

For instance, in the late 1920s, Patrick Henry ("Packy") Lennon sold quantities of dud stock in a company called the Inter-City Radio & Telegraph Corporation. Lennon boosted the value of the stock by spreading the rumor that a couple of big-shot Hollywood producers were lining up to buy the company. Similar scams remain standard today, have indeed burgeoned, because the Internet provides a whole uncontrollable new forum in which such rumor can be spread.

One of Packy Lennon's most enthusiastic customers was Augustine J. Cunningham, an industrialist from Rochester, New York, who invested $107,147.27 in Inter-City, all of which he lost when the company folded in 1930 and Lennon was eventually sent to jail for securities fraud. Whereupon Cunningham promptly forgot about Packy Lennon, but Lennon did not forget about his richest and most obliging sucker.

Following his release, in the early 1950s Lennon devised a scheme to fleece Cunningham again, sending one of his confederates, Otis W. Rowe, aka Donald Peddit, over to Rochester. Rowe/Peddit told Cunningham the story that Packy Lennon had come up with. This legend concerned Dr. Randolph Parker, an inventor at one time connected with Inter-City who had died and left an extraordinary will, bequeathing his estate, the value of which was mostly in patents for movie cameras and electronic technology, to the three investors hardest hit by the collapse of the company. Cunningham was one of them, a man named Harry Hoffman was another, Rowe/Peddit said, and the really good news was that several of Parker's patents had been repeatedly infringed by the big Hollywood studios. The final settlement looked like it would be somewhere in the region of $60 million. In other words, the surprised and delighted Cunningham could expect to get $20 million.

A few weeks later, Rowe/Peddit was back in Rochester, bringing with him Harry Hoffman, a cheerful, neatly attired, wealthy-looking fellow who exchanged commiserations with Cunningham about the way they'd both been taken by the sharpers behind Inter-City. "But all's well that ends well," Hoffman said. "We're in for a windfall now." Then, as E. J. Kahn noted in a 1950s *New Yorker* article, Hoffman grew serious for a moment, informing Cunningham that there might be an "obstacle or two." Those Hollywood studios, after all, were nothing if not clever, and notorious for employing slick and sly lawyers. "We'll have to be patient," Hoffman said, "and prepared to take action ourselves." Discretion was required, he said, and money to defray the necessary expenses. Indeed, he told Cunningham, he'd already been forced to spend quite a lot of money himself, but he thoroughly expected the investment to be worth it.

There were various things about this deal that Cunningham didn't understand or know about, principal among them being that there was no Randolph Parker, and therefore no will, and therefore no patents whose copyright had been infringed and no pending lawsuit with the bigwigs on the coast. Harry Hoffman was actually Packy Lennon in disguise.

Like Chris Rawlings, Lennon had graduated from crude stock fraud to a subtle and more involved version of the Drake scheme. The key twist here was the fictitious Randolph Parker and his fictitious movie camera patents, and the idea that these had been stolen by MGM and Warner Bros. Copyright infringement means attorneys, and attorneys mean money. Everyone gets that. Plus that Hollywood is glamorous and maybe even crooked. So expect delays. Plenty of obstacles. Over a four-year period in the early 1950s, Hoffman persuaded Cunningham to give him $339,121, demonstrating two basic propositions that the cleverest confidence men know and rely on: first, there is no seeming limit to the credulity of a greedy sucker once he's been hooked; second, the moment when a game appears to be all done and worn out, utterly exhausted, might just be the moment when it springs to life and gets interesting again. In this the con man is like Scheherazade in *The Thousand and One Nights*, who understood that a part of us wants a good story never to be over.

⌒

Hartzell made staying in London a big part of his own version of the scheme. He'd been in the city almost six years now and felt more comfortable there than he did back home, seeing in its bustling, foggy streets an anonymity, a simpler opportunity for self-invention than would have been available in Des Moines or New York. The English treated him well, and he liked them. They didn't know he'd been a bankrupt, a failure. To them he was a bluff American with a cigar and a ready laugh. "London," said Henry James, "is on the whole the most possible form of life." Like countless misfits and dreamers and con men and storytellers before and since, Hartzell was starting to make his own London.

He'd found a friend, another American lawyer based in London, a man named Arthur Sylvester Welch, who had been in Milo Lewis's camp but, impressed by Hartzell's performance, had switched sides. Welch, who was ten years older than Hartzell, became his confidant and mentor.

If Hartzell was going to live in London while running the show—and he and Welch agreed that this would be more elegant and much safer too—he needed a steady flow of cash. So he made one more journey to America to set things up. It was a visit that called upon all his salesman's confidence and skills.

In the Great Northern Hotel in Chicago he met with his brothers, Clinton and Canfield, and his sister, Pearl Palmer. Clinton was then a farmer and horse trader in Fairbault, Minnesota, Pearl was married to a Rotarian and living in Galva, Illinois, and the burly Canfield was based in New York, where he was already into his third marriage and had a job that might have come straight from the pages of Damon Runyon, selling memberships to Broadway clubs and speakeasies, letting boobs know about casinos and high-priced floating card games where, most likely, they would be robbed blind. I think we can assume that Canfield already knew something of the sides of life that are less than legal.

Hartzell invited his three siblings to come in with him on the scheme; he offered them jobs, at $10,000 a year (about $100,000 in today's money), or half of what they managed to get collected, and the lounge of the Great Northern Hotel became the scene of a family bust-up. Clinton warned that no good would come of this and they'd all end up in jail. Canfield told Clinton he'd always been a coward and threatened to punch him on the nose. Clinton quickly left, but Canfield and Pearl stayed.

Hartzell explained how the Drake con was going to work now;

the scheme was to have a different structure. Instead of selling shares, they would merely seek donations, with the assurance that when settlement came the donors would get their money back, plus 6 percent compound interest, plus a discretionary bonus, which would be of the order of five hundred to one or even a thousand to one.

Hartzell had figured all this out with Arthur Welch, reckoning that the new idea would make it much more difficult for the law ever to touch any of them—after all, what was illegal about accepting a donation? He showed Canfield and Pearl the receipts he'd had printed up. One of these would be handed to each donor every time he or she gave money. The words "Donated to Oscar Hartzell" would be written on the receipts, which were like checks, with the head of a horned cow peeping out of one corner.

Both Canfield and Pearl agreed to help him; Canfield's role would grow more important as time went on, although it's not clear that Pearl did anything other than provide information and offer moral support.

Hartzell left Chicago for Des Moines, where the trickiest work began. He met with Dr. Charles Cochran, his old partner in the failed real estate venture, and with his friend Alma Shepard, the woman who had been doused by a Lewis backer. Both of them were still believers in the Drake Estate but disenchanted with Whittaker and Lewis. Shepard was a sharp-faced woman of about sixty whose husband had a successful small business—he was one of the best-known tailors in Des Moines. Hartzell saw in her the potential of a lively and determined apostle. They discussed the sad state into which the affairs of the Drake Estate had been plunged. He told her how shocked he'd been by the behavior of Lewis and Whittaker, and how his faith in the deal was nonetheless unshaken, if only it was handled by someone on the level. Alma Shepard replied that she couldn't agree more.

Hartzell made her his chief agent in Iowa, with power to appoint further subagents, and the system was in place whereby the scheme would run from then on. His lieutenants (there would be others after Shepard) would recruit agents in a particular neighborhood, and these men and women would canvass donations, either door-to-door or by organizing meetings, seeking lump sums, and, better yet, money on a weekly or monthly basis. The arrangement was clublike, and Hartzell knew that everyone involved would most likely be skimming money off the top for himself, so he made his requirements clear. He needed $2,500 a week (i.e., about $25,000 in today's terms) every week without fail. "And I must have three things—secrecy, silence, nondisturbance," he said.

With that, having made his arrangements and gained the agreement of Shepard and Cochran, he left Des Moines for Chicago, New York, and then England, where he stayed without leaving for the next eleven years.

The struggle for power with Whittaker and Lewis had been real enough, but Hartzell had observed that it hadn't destroyed belief in the reality of the fortune itself. Rather the confusion had heightened such belief. These people have been fighting, the thinking went, so they must have been fighting about *something*. An additional gloss of credibility had been created, and this in turn produced a need. Having denounced the Rundle U. Upham genealogy on which Sudie Whittaker relied and declared the notion that the Roarchport Drakes were Sir Francis's true descendants to be "fraudulent and impossible," Hartzell was in search of a plausible alternative. In Chicago he'd organized the nuts and bolts, engineered how the money would flow. Now he had to create a moving force, the idea that would make the machine spin. It was a matter of urgency at this point—he needed an heir.

In 1936 a prison psychiatrist wrote:

> For one who had spent his life in terms of the possible acquirement of money and property, as Hartzell had done, it must have been painful to have seen others get so large a slice of the melon. He had quarreled long and bitterly with both Mrs. Whittaker and Lewis, and obviously there was little love to be lost, if he were to turn his back upon them and attempt to reap the whole harvest himself. This did not call for any great amount of original thinking; he had a complete pattern before him which had been in operation for years and its shortcomings were apparent. It was only necessary to erect a promotion similar to the Whittaker-Lewis plan, and make bigger and better promises, and make available less tangible information.

This is what Hartzell did, although I think that the psychiatrist did him a disservice in saying he showed no originality. Hartzell was like a writer of mysteries or thrillers, reconfiguring the plot. He had a tried and tested theme in front of him but required some special twist that would make his own version of the story play. What he came up with was indeed original, a dazzling sideways leap, an idea both outrageous and inspired—not to mention megalomaniacal.

⁓

The story comes back to Joy Broadburn. In 1934, after she'd sent her letter to prosecutor Harry Reed, after the trial in Sioux City, she gave a statement and spoke in more detail both about her own life and about her relationship with Hartzell. She said that as a young girl she'd been adopted by relatives who lived in the west of England, where Sir Francis Drake had made his home. Here she met another Francis Drake, in fact the last living English descendant of the great man, who lived with his sister in a charming little house called Rose Cottage. Broadburn, who was about thirteen at the time, became so friendly with the couple that the sister asked her brother, Francis, to make a will in her favor. This was the will that, years later, Broadburn handed to Oscar Hartzell, who in his bullish way went ahead and opened it, and then sped west to see Francis Drake, hoping to induce him to sign a deed making over whatever rights he might have in the Drake Estate. Francis Drake said he would sign nothing unless he got £750. Hartzell persuaded Joy Broadburn to draw £500 from her savings account, because he had only £250 himself. With this money Hartzell did get Francis Drake to sign the deed, which he then locked up in a safety deposit box at the Selfridges department store, along with the will Broadburn had given him, promising that he would share the fortune with her when he got it.

This, to repeat, is the story Joy Broadburn told in 1934. At that time it wasn't examined closely, or even presented in court; it was merely another piece of evidence in a big pile demonstrating that Oscar Hartzell was a rogue. The story is a self-justifying fabrication, made at a time when Hartzell was discredited in the eyes of the law and Broadburn both wanted to get back at him and to protect herself from the possibility of prosecution. There's about as much truth in it as in Hartzell's tale about the gold mine, the amorous woman, and the man hiding under the bed—which is to say that it's a lie with a clue at its core. What's important here is the gimmick of *another will*. Either Broadburn or Hartzell or the two of them in bed together came up with this idea, and Hartzell seized upon it, perceiving that it was just what he needed to begin constructing a version of the Drake Estate scheme that would stand independent of Sudie Whittaker's now that she and Lewis were on the ropes.

Hartzell recognized that another will implied the possibility of another, hitherto unknown heir, and so he dreamed up a narrative to explain how he'd found such a will, and what this will meant. He wrote to Dr. Charles Cochran and explained how he had been befriended in London by Lady Curzon. This was a nice touch: Lady Curzon was eminent, but on the other hand he wasn't claiming friendship with Queen Mary—the judgment was just right. He said that Lady Curzon, on learning of his interest in the Drake Estate, had told him about the existence of a secret and suppressed will, and had promised to help him. He was to join her for morning service at a church in Devon and watch her eyes. He did so, and saw Lady Curzon frequently raise her glance upward. That Sunday night, at midnight, he broke into the church and climbed the stairs to the belfry, where, delving among old papers covered six inches deep in dust, he found the will.

"The will proved that Sir Francis Drake, unknown to everyone, married for a third time and did in fact have a son," Cochran later told a reporter. "Hartzell established that this son was Drake's heir, and traced the line down to Colonel Drexel Drake in London."

The details were, to say the least, farfetched; on the other hand they were quite in keeping with the murky air in which Whittaker and Lewis had cloaked everything about the English side of the Drake Estate. Once again, Hartzell showed that beneath the mask of the tough businessman lay another identity, that of an adventurer with a gift for outrageous wish-fulfilling fantasy.

The fiction gave him a whole new Drake lineage, an heir with no connection to any previous claimant, and to this he now added a decisive twist. On April 25, 1924, he went to Trafalgar Square, to the offices of the *Chicago Daily News,* and revealed his hand in a letter to a Des Moines attorney who was handling his American legal affairs.

He began:

> Well I am going to write you the letter you have been looking for for months and which I have written three times but destroyed and would not let ride thinking it was not the thing to do under the conditions, my mail having been opened and destroyed and misdirected in the past. . . . I am going to take the chance on opening the gates to you so you can understand matters as they are and my success.

He explained what had been going on since the discovery of the new will.

> In the latter days of June my genealogy was presented to the King & Crown's Commission which is the highest in the British Empire and the only and last place that a case of this kind can be finished and their decision is final and cannot be attacked in the courts or by anybody and after they have finished up on the matter it is *finished for ever.*

He said that his genealogy had been established and checked in the last part of July 1923, confirming Colonel Drexel Drake as the rightful heir to the baronetcy, and therefore the estate. "The baronetcy and the seals are ready for delivery and have been since last August," he wrote, "and I have been in full power since then."

This was all invention: there was no such thing as the "King & Crown's Commission," Colonel Drexel Drake did not exist, and he,

Hartzell, had made no application claiming the baronetcy and estate in front of any kind of British court. Figuring he'd better not stay with the fictional detail for too long, he switched to something he knew to be true—the disarray existing in the Whittaker/Lewis camp. On this he was both irreverent and convincing. He could afford to exaggerate and yet still be believed.

> Lewis and Whittaker were having dinner at the hotel where she was staying and he had a brainstorm and threw a wine bottle at her and broke up plates, whereupon the hotel man had him summoned for damages. In court Lewis gave his name as some other name and had to pay damages and costs and was told not to leave the country. Two weeks later he was running with a lady that was working in one of the large stores over here. He got jealous of the manager and went up to the manager and took another brainstorm and struck the manager. The manager had him summoned and they was a month getting that settled. Some time back he had got another man's daughter into trouble and he was in a public place consulting with a lawyer and the father of this girl came into the place. He and Lewis got into a mix up and the man told him that he had until Monday morning to pay him 250 pounds or about $1000. This lawyer got scared and left at once so that Lewis had to get another lawyer but I understand he paid the $1000. He has a *herd* of illegitimate children.

Hartzell knew he was safe, gloating over the Keystone Cops escapades now befalling the defeated Milo Lewis, and he stressed that at all costs he wished to avoid such chaos himself. This meant he had to be left alone.

I want you to read this letter to parties that you know you can trust. Also I want you to warn anybody who is my supporter that there is one thing that has to be stopped and if it is not stopped I will go through them so hard they will never find bottom— that is this trying to verify my statements and check up on me just to satisfy their dirty filthy minds. Enough is enough of anything and I have had enough of mess and embarrassment with that Whittaker and Lewis crowd. Why, a shipload of money and a shipload of lawyers from Iowa would not amount to a snap of your fingers over here in this deal. I want Mrs. Shepard to be very firm from now on with people that are not satisfied. I don't want any whining from anybody. The hell with what they think—I am the man that is making them their money.

This eighteen-page letter to his Iowa attorney was a swirl of fantasy, fact, persuasion, obfuscation, and outright abuse; but everything thus far had been mere preamble, cover for the crucial point that was about to come.

I will try and explain so I think you can understand. Since August they have been getting all the details ready to demand everything that follows the title under the law of today that was passed 30 or 40 years ago which gives the rightful heir the right to *transfer all property* and everything that follows the title to anybody he choses *not by will but by deed*. That has been done. Everything has been transferred, signed, seal by the heir to myself.

He'd made this agreement with Colonel Drexel Drake, he said, during the month of February 1923, and since then had had many sleepless nights, lest the colonel die or change his mind before the assignment was ratified by the British government and the British legal authorities. But now that had happened, he was secure; when the Drake Estate was settled, everything—all the jewels, all the treasure, all the lands, all the gold, all the investments—would come to him as though he were the heir, because the heir had assigned him the rights to everything.

This was Hartzell's breakthrough, an idea so blunt and far-reaching a part of him must have wondered whether his American public would fall for it; but, stated with such angry and inspired conviction, it proved a masterstroke, simplifying everything. No one had to bother anymore about the Rev. Bampfield or Bamfield Drake, or the lost three brothers Drake (one of whom had hunted with Daniel Boone in Kentucky), or Ernest Drake, or even Colonel Drexel Drake himself, because the heir was, in effect, Oscar Hartzell. Once the estate was settled it would all belong to him. Why had Colonel Drexel Drake made a gesture of such extraordinary generosity? Why had he agreed to hand over his rights to the fortune? Hartzell was ready with the answer. He'd met Colonel Drexel Drake's niece, he said, and she'd fallen in love with him, and they were to be married; in assigning the Drake Estate over to him Colonel Drake was merely keeping everything in the family.

Hartzell also suggested that Queen Elizabeth had taken more than her due from the *Golden Hind* on Drake's return to England in 1580 and that he would be seeking restitution from the British government. At least some of this money was rightfully part of Drake's estate too, he argued, and had been accumulating compound interest ever since.

Everything was going to be an awful lot of money:

Figure up all the land in Missouri, Kansas, and Iowa at an average of $125 an acre, and all of the stocks, and all the bank deposits, all the railroads and cities in those three states and add them together and the combined amount would not be as large as the Sir Francis Drake estate here in England, of which I am the sole owner, and to which I hold the sole title, which the British parliament is now conveying to me in cash, and which I am going to bring to America to distribute among the men and women who have advanced me money with which to carry on the money to win this estate.

When I get this money, and I expect to get it in the summer, I could buy the three states of Missouri, Kansas and Iowa, every foot of land and every dollar's worth of property in them, and put a fence around the whole lot and then have more gold left over than all of you ever dreamed of.

I will put it before you in another form: it has been said by people of high finance here in London that the amount I am to receive from the sale of the Drake is considerably more than the combined debt of Britain to the United States, and the debts of all other countries to Great Britain, and that, as you can read for yourselves, is over four and a half billion pounds sterling, or some 20 billion dollars, a stake worth fighting for and working for and waiting for.

Hartzell's Scotland Yard file, MEPO 3/2765 (MEPO is short for Metropolitan Police), resides at the British Public Records Office in Kew, and I went there to look at it. The earliest piece of material in the file was his first immigration card, dating from his arrival in England in 1916. Next was a 1919 letter from the office of a colonel at MI5 (British military intelligence) asking Scotland Yard to look into what was known of an American named Oscar Hartzell. There was no suggestion that Hartzell might actually have been a spy, but he was a foreigner with a German-sounding name who was in the habit of traveling to and fro across the Atlantic, and MI5 wanted to know more about him. Scotland Yard's reply, which went into the Home Office filing system, had not been kept, but the MI5 letter led to MEPO 3/2765 being sealed under the terms of the British Official Secrets Act, and the file had remained closed until I applied to have it opened.

The file was full of fascinating things. It showed, for instance, how close Hartzell came to being shut down before he really got going in England. In 1922 he was the subject of a complaint from Mrs. N. Scheid, who met him on a boat coming to Southampton and gave him $50 for two shares in the Drake Estate and never received share certificates. She asked for her money back and didn't get that either. An unnamed Yard detective added a dry footnote to Scheid's letter: "This is very 'fishy.' Although we can do nothing to prevent credulous Americans putting money into this bogus concern, we might interview Hartzell and ask for some explanation of his obviously bogus claims." An officer (the first of many who would make Hartzell's acquaintance) was duly sent to pay a call, and Hartzell told him that Mrs. Scheid had got this all wrong—in fact she was the one who owed him money. The Yard man, impressed by Hartzell's righteous anger, recommended no further action.

The next complaint came not from a credulous American but from a ranking officer in the British army. Major E. F. Ross wrote from the Hotel Hammerand in Vienna, telling how Hartzell had sold him shares in London and had promised to lodge the certificates in the safe depository at Selfridges. This hadn't happened, and now Major Ross, like the hopeful Mrs. Scheid, wanted his money back. He said he had written to Hartzell, but Hartzell's attitude had been "quite indifferent." Ross concluded his sorry tale with bluster: "Hartzell is an *American*," he wrote, as if this settled everything.

Another Yard man was sent over, but again Hartzell said he was the one who had been swindled and no action was taken.

Hartzell was lucky, and we see here how short of cash, how close to the edge, he must have been in London at one time. In 1922, even after breaking with Whittaker and Lewis, he was selling shares as if he were still involved with the old version of the scheme. He was risking everything, working the short con (i.e., making a quick hit for an immediate gain he didn't expect to repeat), and he was almost caught. It was an important lesson: never again would he try to get any stranger in England to invest in, or donate to, his venture. After a while, he didn't need to.

Records kept by American Express tell the story of how his business gained momentum. In the month of April 1924 he received a little under £452 by wire, or about $2,250 ($22,500 in today's money); in July 1925 it was £1,435, more than $7,000; and by September 1926 the sum had risen to £1,650 or so, more than $8,000 ($80,000).

Meanwhile the wires he sent in return, those he sent back to Iowa, fizzed with self-importance and conviction. He preached. He commanded. His tone of authority impelled his readers to believe that he was indeed dealing with the "highest powers that be," "the King's and Lords' Commission," and "the Ecclesiastical Courts." He didn't, couldn't, tell his donors what they most wanted to hear, that the money—all those billions—was really on its way; he was constantly telling them the next best thing, that it would be coming very, very soon.

In the letter of April 1924 to his attorney he'd promised that the British government would be delivering the money later that summer. At first it was easy for him to explain why this didn't happen. The entire Drake Estate had to be audited and accounted for. This meant adding up the value of the many and various properties that were involved; it meant transferring the titles to those properties from the people who thought they were in rightful possession to the British government before those titles could then be given to him; it meant calculating the portion of the estate that the British government itself was holding (plus all that compound interest); it meant accounting for every tree and load of timber that had been cut off Drake's lands since his death; it meant figuring out the value of "all rock quarries, brick yards, pottery clay, mineral ores, such as tin etc., fishing rights in rivers, income off railroad land, and all rents from properties, which have been accumulating all these years"; it meant counting every gold coin, assessing the value of every gem, and certain streets and important buildings in London. There was land in Africa, in Alaska, in Australia, in continental Europe, in South America, as well as in Virginia and California and England. The British were actively engaged in repossessing all this so it could be turned over to him; even the Muir Valley redwoods were a part of it.

This tortured process was "drawing up the balance sheet"; and once the basic proposition of the swindle was accepted—that the value of everything to do with the estate of Sir Francis Drake for the last three hundred years had to be calculated and then reassigned—you could see easily why it might take a lot of time, lawyers, and, therefore, money. If anything was wrong, if any of the seals on the document were wrong, or any of the ribbons that were held by the seals were not tied right or cut in the right shape, then that could nix the whole deal. It took reams and reams of special parchment paper, Hartzell said.

On December 10, 1924, his mother, Emma, died. Hartzell didn't go back for the funeral, but in Monmouth at that time Canfield and Clinton Hartzell had another angry confrontation about the Drake Estate, with Clinton warning, again, "You'll all end up in the slammer." This was reported to Hartzell by his sister, Pearl, but he told her not to worry about it. In his wire he also referred to the money he'd been sending her, for her family and the upkeep and education of her daughter. He warned: "Don't go lording it about, buying cars, otherwise you might get us all in a jam."

Somehow word got out. In Des Moines the tenacious Alma Shepard didn't suspect that the Drake Estate was a fraud, but she began to think that Oscar Hartzell was. At the beginning of 1925 she hired a private detective, who traveled to London and trailed Hartzell, reporting back on where he went and whom he met. Alma Shepard wasn't satisfied by what she heard. Defying Hartzell's angry edicts, his demands for silence and noninterference, she traveled to London herself to confront him. Possibly she was making a play for control of the scheme. Most likely she was just fed up. She wanted him to take her to meet Colonel Drexel Drake and his niece. Hartzell, of course, was unable to oblige. There was no Colonel Drexel Drake, let alone a niece. He told Alma Shepard that such a meeting was out of the question—the colonel met only with him.

"I went to London and hunted Hartzell out, found him wearing a thousand-dollar diamond, living in a rich apartment, and spending as much as $100 on one dinner for his friends," Shepard said later. "But he wouldn't show me what I wanted to see—Colonel Drake. Nor did he show me any evidence that there was a Drake Estate. He did take me into the vaults of the Bank of England and show me big bags, like potato sacks, filled with coins, which he said were Spanish doubloons and pieces-of-eight which Drake had captured and that belonged to the Drake Estate."

On her return to Des Moines she denounced Hartzell as a fraud; two of her subagents, both women, sprang to Hartzell's defense, and Alma Shepard had them run out of town.

But Hartzell was on his mettle now. His response was swift and hot-tempered and clever. He wrote a letter to I. T. Jones, the Iowa attorney, and told Jones to circulate the letter widely around Des Moines. He promised that his new enemy Alma Shepard was going to be prosecuted both civilly and criminally.

> I have fully made up my mind to this, and I shall spend $100,000 or even $1m to achieve this object if I have to. I think it is an absolute scandal that two ladies should be forced to leave their home because they were my co-workers. What a bunch of skunks they must be, Shepard and her criminal gang to try and cover up their criminal work. . . . I shall double those women's donations for what they have had to go through on account of wicked, cunning, crooked old reprobate Shepard and her criminal gang. I want you all to understand my position is such that it makes me absolutely fearless in regard to what I am going to say, for my statements are absolutely correct.

Nor was he through yet. He launched a counterplot, alleging that Shepard and her husband were thieves, having withheld $75,000 of the $166,775 they had collected for him. Dr. Charles Cochran and his brother Canfield had checked secretly through Shepard's accounts—monies indeed were missing, he said. Now it was the Shepards who found themselves the subject of ugly gossip and rumor. They were cold-shouldered, ostracized, in Des Moines.

Hartzell said everybody would have to take sides. It was either Oscar Hartzell or Alma Shepard, and he warned ominously that anyone who went with her would find his or her name crossed through with red ink on the roll of donors. He made this sound like the threat of doom itself. "Now people I played that Mrs. Shepard good and proper," he wrote. "They have a fine chance, haven't they? The whole bunch of crooks will sneak off like dogs. . . ."

Alma Shepard was no match for Hartzell in this area. Her life was destroyed: her merchant tailor husband, once proud, was hit so hard by their disgrace that he had to be committed to the Iowa state asylum at Clarinda, and died soon after.

"Hartzell reduced me to poverty, drove my husband insane, and here I am, a widow, with just a few dollars left me by my sister, living alone in one room," Shepard said. She joined Milo Lewis and Sudie Whittaker in the ranks of those who, at the mention of the name Oscar Hartzell, found themselves fuming with hate.

In his autobiography Hartzell reflected on this episode without qualm. The aged Alma Shepard, led astray by greed, had gotten what was coming to her, he said. He was ever resourceful, but not a charitable winner, and he really did possess the chilly ruthlessness of the money barons he so admired. Success wasn't the main thing, it was the only thing. He wrote: "I traveled alone. I was not afraid of the devil, man, or beast, or any place or anywhere. I had no fear and had not until this day. No man could stand up to me for I was always big enough to master any situation. I always got there in the end."

That settled that.

⌒

He dressed the part of a rich man, sometimes swaggering down Piccadilly in a Stetson, as if he really were a Texas millionaire abroad, footloose and fancy free in a cowboy hat; other times he favored spats, monocle, and cane, practicing the part of an English toff. He took elocution lessons and learned to dance. His writing style improved notably—under the guidance and influence of his friend Arthur Sylvester Welch. He whiled away the afternoons with manicures, massages, and pampering himself for the night ahead. For a while, in 1922, he'd been living with Eunice Colliss, but by the end of 1923 he'd moved out again and had three flats he was keeping in various parts of the city. Joy Broadburn remembered meeting him in one and being introduced to an artist's model named Dolores, to whom he was giving money. In Maida Vale he rented rooms from a couple, husband and wife, vaudeville jugglers, and when the wife had her baby in the middle of the night it was Hartzell who went and found the doctor. His life had taken an exotic turn.

Came the day when he cajoled Joy Broadburn into parting with her ruby ring and her diamond horseshoe brooch. Later, in effervescent mood, he told her that he had indeed met King George V at Buckingham Palace and he had the signature of Lord Cave, the lord chancellor, and the case had passed the House of Lords and the king himself had stated they were going to pay him billions at an early date. He then produced some old parchment from his pocket, but refused to let her touch it. He really began to build financial castles in the air, telling her he intended to buy out American Express and set her up on a ranch in Kentucky. Joy Broadburn laughed at this nonsense, but was pleased, and Hartzell said he hoped to marry her.

In time he gave up the other places he was renting and took an apartment in a handsome mansion block on Basil Street in swanky Knightsbridge. He came literally closer to the center of things. He started having his suits made on Savile Row. He dined so often at the Savoy that he had a regular table there, number 101. He moved in a nighttime London that, like New York, swayed to the dashing rhythms of jazz. His world was dressing for dinner, unstinted champagne, and nightclubs where he watched with amusement the antics of smooth young men and ravishing young women. This was the sort of glamour he'd dreamed about. In wires and letters he sent back to America he was referring to himself, grandly, as Baron Buckland, though Joy Broadburn advised him not to try to get away with this in London. A Scotland Yard man who tailed him for several months gave a rueful and envious account of this American scoundrel at work, or—as it seemed—at his leisure, in any event at the top of his game. Detective Sergeant George Page wrote:

> I kept observation on the movements of Hartzell and found them to be monotonously regular. Hartzell left his flat every morning at about 10.20. He invariably purchased four cigars at the tobacconists at Knightsbridge Station. He travelled by Underground from Knightsbridge to Piccadilly and sometimes took a cab for the short distance from the station to the American Express offices. He would then go straight to the library, meet his friends and confederates. He usually remained at the American Express Office until about 12 noon.
>
> On a number of occasions I went into the library and saw Hartzell reading cablegrams and sometimes writing on cable forms. I have also seen him draw large sums of money from the cashier. From the American Express, he invariably went to the Carlton Hotel Lounge and consumed expensive drinks. He always left the Carlton about 1 pm, had lunch at a high class restaurant, and arrived home about 3.30 pm. He would reappear about 6.30 pm to 7 pm in evening dress and would dine at the Berkeley or Savoy Hotel. I have seen him treated with the greatest deference by the hall porters at both these establishments and also at the Kit-Kat Club, when he has entered, sometimes accompanied by one or more splendidly dressed women.

At the Kit-Kat Club that other great man about town, Edward Windsor, Prince of Wales, was sometimes to be seen, bashing the drums behind a jazz orchestra. Like Drake before him, Hartzell had risen in the world and was rubbing shoulders with royalty.

Authorities on both sides of the Atlantic helped him by bungling their responses to the swindle. As early as August 9, 1922, the British Home Office had written to the American embassy in London, confirming that there was no unclaimed Sir Francis Drake Estate. This pronouncement, widely circulated by the State Department, only played into Hartzell's hands. He wired his donors, happily acknowledging the fact. Indeed, he said, there was no such item as "an unclaimed Sir Francis Drake Estate." His point was quite different, namely that the estate was legally in the hands of the wrong people and should be handed over to Colonel Drexel Drake and thus himself. Late in 1924 the State Department wrote to Scotland Yard asking whether anything could be done about Oscar Hartzell. Scotland Yard wrote back saying that numerous complaints had been received about Hartzell's activities but nothing could be done because he was committing no offense in England. Responsibility was lobbed back in the direction of the State Department in Washington, which in turn merely kept issuing the British Home Office's statement of 1922—to no useful effect. For years bureaucrats in both England and America couldn't, or wouldn't, get a grip on the case. By day he was like a bar of soap, slipping between the fingers of two jurisdictions; at night, mingling with his women and the bright young things and the heir to the throne, he was in his pomp.

—

The earliest analysis in English of how con men work occurs in the work of Robert Greene, best known to us today as William Shakespeare's first critic. In 1592 the rowdy-living Greene accused Shakespeare of plagiarism and dubbed him "an upstart crow, beautified with our feathers." As Greene was dying at the time, the spitting envy was understandable, and at least it was launched in the direction of a genius so unspeakably prodigious he probably did baffle and gall any other writer who was forced to bow before him. Greene knew that a younger, a more professional, and a much, much greater talent had arrived on the scene and was snatching the playwriting commissions that had been his. Greene, a con man and double-dealer himself, had once sold the same play twice, to the Queen's Players and the Lord Admiral's Men, two of the great rival theatrical groups in Elizabethan England. This probably didn't endear him to his producers, who knew him as "a rakehell, a makeshift, a scribbling fool, a desperate Dick." Now, in 1591 and 1592, crawling with lice and kidneys rotting, coming to a sticky end, he was reduced to churning out gossip (hence the dig at Shakespeare) and hack journalism about London's slang and humor and low life.

Like many subsequent studies of the con, Greene's two short pamphlets about the "cony-catchers" (a cony being a rabbit, as in ready to lose its pelt) and the longer *A Notable Discovery of Cozenage* (cozenage: cheating, deception, fraud) were ostensibly warnings, carefully detailing the means and methods of "the Fetcher, the Shifter, the Ruffler, the Prigger, the Cross-Biter, the Nip, the Foist, and the Deceits of their Doxies" for the benefit of the unwary. Actually they were written less to keep human rabbits from being skinned than out of Greene's delight in a subject he knew so well and his need for quick cash so he could buy wine. In consequence they were inventive and lively. They had pace and bustle.

One of Greene's tricksters avowed his creed: "As my religion is small, so my devotion is less—the two ends I aim at are gain and ease." Greene also blurred the distinction between victim and con man by making the cony, in intention, as great a rogue as his catcher, an attitude that prefigured Yellow Kid Weil's self-justifying statement of more than three hundred years later: "You can't cheat an honest man." This is, of course, untrue. Honest men get cheated all the time—if they're trusting, or none too clever, or unlucky, or greedy, etc. But Greene's conies wanted something for nothing, and what they got was Weil's inevitable nothing for something, and they were given this through ruses and schemes that were in essence those we know today as three-card monte, the shell game, the gold-brick fraud, the estate swindle, and so on. Only the trappings and superficial details were different.

A reading of Greene also shows that the dramatic structure of the grift is unchanged. Each con is like an unfolding story. Greene broke the play carefully down into its component acts. There was the finding and roping of the cony; there was the telling and selling of the scheme; there was the payoff. And there was another stage, when things changed, or went wrong, and the cony-catcher skipped out, or, if he was clever and nimble enough, adjusted himself to the situation so that not only was he safe, but the cony was persuaded to come back with more money. He conjured the circumstances in which the scam went on, and on.

This is the Scheherazade factor, what Packy Lennon had in mind when he told his dupe that there might be "an obstacle or two." Robert Greene had another name for this stage of the con. He called it "the misrule."

All the psychiatrists who later examined Oscar Hartzell concluded that he was of below-average intelligence, even stupid. In some ways, from the point of view of certain kinds of tests, this may be true, but it fails to explain how abnormally apt Hartzell was in certain other areas, how he was able to rake in so much money, beat out so many people so much cleverer than he was, and keep the Drake scheme in the air for so long. Certainly he was often blunt, brazen, and crude. Even with the help of Arthur Welch he never quite acquired the polish of Sudie Whittaker and Milo Lewis; nor did he have the moxie and smarts that the average street hustler needs to survive. Had he been running the Drake Estate swindle in

America, the pressure of being near to his dupes would have been too much for him. Yet in London, with the safety of distance, he was different. In London, when any problem with the Drake con came up, he was sharp, and if not quick, keenly perceptive about what was required. In London, under pressure, he could create. Having to fight and come up with an idea broke through the fog of everything else. Nothing spurred his intelligence like the threat of exposure. He only needed to feel this when he went to American Express on the Haymarket every morning to collect his money and reply to his mail and messages. Only then did he have to step out of his role as the moneyed clubman and become Honest Oscar, the onetime plowboy who was laboring night and day to wrest billions from the British government. It was as if the situation acted on him like a temporary drug. His imagination began to boil and he became a showman.

He invented, for instance, a Scotland Yard detective named Mogford (sometimes also referred to as Mogford-Blythe), a friend, it seemed, of the nephew of the English insurance man Owen, who lived in Des Moines. Mogford wrote a letter to Owen. That's to say, Hartzell typed a letter to Owen, and somebody else, Arthur Welch probably, signed the name Mogford at the bottom of it. The letter disclosed how Scotland Yard had been warned to look out for Hartzell as soon as he arrived in England back in 1916 because he was running with two known crooks named Milo Lewis and Sudie Whittaker. But now, Mogford went on, the Yard had discovered that Hartzell had broken ranks with those notorious bad hats and had started out on his own line, a different line entirely. This was the first time, Mogford said, that he and his detective colleagues had seen the true and staunch character of this man Oscar Hartzell, who was swimming in deep and tricky waters but had powerful friends. Mogford wanted to be especially clear about this because he knew there were stories around Des Moines that Oscar wasn't using the money as he should; these stories were lies, Mogford assured Owen, because Hartzell's friends were of the best.

He also invented an agreement he claimed Lord Cave had signed. Lord Cave was the lord chancellor, the highest legal authority in England, "the man that sits on the woolsack," as Hartzell described him, the equivalent of the chief justice of the Supreme Court. The agreement said: "His Majesty and those who represent His Majesty will deliver at most possible speed all the lands, deeds, title deeds, monies, cumulations and personal effects of the Drake Estate to the said Oscar Merrill Hartzell, who becomes British subject and Sir Francis Drake at time of delivery." Many people in England were very unhappy that Lord Cave had signed this document, Hartzell said, and to be on the safe side from the legal point of view he'd had Cave sign two versions of it, both of which were safe in a strongbox.

He aired out, quite casually, that the secret third wife of Sir Francis Drake had been the highest-ranking lady in England and her name began with an E; in other words, she was Queen Elizabeth herself, although to dare say so explicitly was to risk prosecution for treason. This was all casual, playful stuff. His real inventive powers were reserved for a form of discourse that became extremely familiar to him: the excuse. He'd announced late in 1925 that the great task of drawing up "the balance sheet," the listing of the entire value of the Drake Estate, had been completed; this list, moreover, had been inspected and approved by the Lord and King's Commission, the Ecclesiastical Courts, all the Powers That Be. So just why hadn't all that money that was going to enable him to buy the states of Missouri, Kansas, and Iowa and put a fence around them been handed over yet? What was going on? Forever thereafter he had to keep coming up with explanations as to why settlement had not been made.

Such as, on June 4, 1926:

The King of England has been working upon the transfer of these titles to me until he has been stricken down with sickness, and we must wait until he recovers to resume work, and all this waiting takes money, so tell our people in the West who have so nobly contributed of their funds in the past that the machinery must not stop over here now, but they must send more money, and keep on sending it, until the transfers are made. I must have $6,000 more by the end of the month, without fail.

In November 1927 he wrote: "Settlement delayed for a month. Estate will be handed over with as much speed as His Majesty can conveniently allow."

On June 29, 1928, it was:

The new Lord Chancellor, who succeeded Lord Cave, and who has the matter in charge to finish, has had to go through the papers to finish the deal. In doing so he discovered an error which was a very close point, as it was with the late Lord Chancellor, but this has been thrashed out and settled.

In consequence of this, however, certain papers and charts will have to be made out afresh to rectify the error in turning over to me certain monies and properties.

This is being done at the utmost possible speed, and immediately they are finished, the settlement will be made.

I also wish to mention that the making out of these new

papers, and charts, means a benefit to me of an additional 250,000 sterling, which is equivalent to about $1,200,000. Plainly understand it does not make any difference whether it is 10,000,000 sterling for me or against me, it has just got to be correct, according to the Lord Chancellor's decision.

A particular friend of mine, who knows all about the affair, when he heard of this remarked: "Oh well, it is just another example of O.M.'s luck again."

This last paragraph, with its jaunty invention of "a particular friend of mine," and that dashing throwaway "O.M.," summoning a vision of Hartzell laughing and rubbing shoulders with the lazily elegant and wealthy denizens of the English upper class, is especially good. He called upon his own deeply felt fantasies of grandeur to give believable spine to the fictions he spun.

In a slightly different vein:

A friend of mine was having tea with a friend of Cave's, Ramsay MacDonald, and the Drake affair rose in conversation, whereupon MacDonald said: "Fancy a cattle man coming over here from the west of America and putting a concrete roof over the British Government and then putting up iron gates and having them locked so nothing could break the deal open."

Here he depicted the Old World trumped and outsmarted by the New's fearless can-do spirit: he was an Iowa cowboy at the court of King George, an idea he knew would have appeal. Like all great con men he was creating theater, a believable yet entirely illusory world, and he plucked its dominant imaginative fabric—the contingency, the chance event—from the air around him. He listened to the radio and to gossip at the American Express and in the clubs where he drank and the restaurants where he ate. He studied the newspapers keenly. King George V was sick? It was because the Drake situation was giving him pains in the stomach and keeping him awake at night. The American ambassador had been recalled to Washington? Naturally, it was to discuss this all-important Drake matter. England was rumored to come off the gold standard? Because, of course, there was panic at the Bank of England concerning this matter of $10 billion, $20 billion, $40 billion, $100 billion (he began steadily to inflate the figure) that was soon to leave British shores for America.

When the inevitable questions kept coming—Where's the money? Why haven't we got the money yet?—he was always ready with an answer. He excelled at improvising, at taking stray threads of news and weaving them into his continuing narrative of delay and demand. He was good when things went wrong. He was used to it. He just kept increasing the odds. Within this one area of his life—the Drake Estate, his imposture—he was a survivor armed with an especially acute sensitivity.

Every little change in the atmosphere was attributable to a scheme whose vast scope and inclusiveness he said he himself sometimes had to struggle to understand. Even the pope was helping him. And yet, somehow, even with the pope's assistance, settlement was never made.

He became a master of the misrule.

⌣

No examination or analysis of Hartzell himself can wholly explain why the story of the Drake Estate swindle turned into such a long-running performance. In London he was a clever and driven impostor whose ambition ticked incessantly; but in America there was an

unguessed-at receptivity to his trickery. Even he couldn't have predicted, or dreamed of, the extent to which the swindle would come
to seem so perfectly designed for the eras it spanned. His scores of
thousands of Midwestern donors (one State Department official
reckoned there were as many as 200,000, although 70,000 to 80,000
is a more likely figure) were not merely his gulls. In the ferocity of
their desire and eagerness to believe, they became his unconscious
conspirators. At first this was mostly to do with the time. America
presupposes an optimistic view of itself and life's possibilities, especially the possibility of getting rich, and in the 1920s that boisterous
self-belief reached a dizzy new height of delusion.

"What is the finest game? Business. The soundest science? Business.
The truest art? Business. The fullest education? Business. The fairest
opportunity? Business. The cleanest philanthropy? Business. The sanest
religion? Business. The rewards are for all, and all can win," wrote
one booster. Easy money was the sermon of the era. Jesus Christ himself was brought into the game. A big best-seller of 1925 was Bruce
Barton's *The Man Nobody Knows*, which touted Christ as a modern,
money-making paradigm, "a virile go-getting he-man of business, a
champion publicity getter, the most popular dinner guest in Jerusalem
who picked twelve men from the bottom ranks and forged a great
organization."

Con men flourish in such times, boom times, times like our own
recent times when getting rich and being rich seem not only desir-
able but moral requirements. In the second decade of the eighteenth
century, as the seemingly limitless potential of the South Sea Company in England gripped the popular imagination, innumerable
other companies, aptly called bubbles, started up. Each morning produced new ventures. Most were established merely with the view of
raising shares in the market. The promoters took the first opportunity of a rise to sell out and the next day they shut down. All of

which sounds very much like the dot-com mania of the late 1990s. Back in 1717 one scheme was a wheel for perpetual motion. Another was "a company for carrying on an undertaking of great advantage, but nobody to know what it is." The enterprising fellow who set up this one collected £2,000 in five hours, left England for France, and was never heard of again.

The 1920s were likewise a gala of scam. Implausible yet unstoppable schemes blossomed like confetti on Lindbergh's parade. Chicago swindlers sold shares in the League of Nations, as though this upright conjoining of countries against war was a business wheeze like any other. Charles Ponzi for a while lived the very high life, drawing in as much as $2 million a day, through the simple expedient of borrowing from his present investors to pay his past ones. Hundreds of itinerant Russian immigrants invested $500,000 in a fictitious gold and platinum mine on the Hudson River. Millions of dollars disappeared into fraudulent Texan oil well ventures. Investors purchased uninspected wetland that turned out actually to be under the Mississippi, property that witty con men advertised as already having running water. In 1926, New Yorkers alone lost $500 million to crooked promoters, bogus brokers, and fake security salesmen. Traveling throughout America, the suave Czech con man Victor Lustig made a fortune selling machines that apparently made $1,000 bills. At certain times, it appears, people will believe anything.

We shouldn't laugh about this. The psychologist William James divided people into the tender-minded and tough-minded, and money—the idea of money, the promise of money, proximity to money—tends to turn the latter into the former, with doses of hope and fear thrown in. We like to think we're clever about money, but most of us aren't; even very educated people can have a hard enough time understanding the concepts of economics and investment, of pure money, without having to make a judgment about whether those who pose as the real experts might in fact be peddling snake oil.

In the 1920s it was so easy for the con man because the old rules for acquiring wealth did not apply. The writer Alva Johnston told how during the Florida land boom they had to beat suckers away with clubs precisely because there were many verifiable tales of instant riches attained and kept—$1 million picked up by a barber, a $350 lot sold three months later for $1.75 million, $20,000 parlayed into $9 million, an eleven-year-old who made $100,000. Johnston said that "the writers Ben Hecht and J. P. McEvoy traveled to Florida to get gags for a W. C. Fields laugh riot about the crazy supersalesmen of rapidly growing nonexistent cities. They forgot W. C. Fields and became supersalesmen themselves of one of the most stupendous of all the rapidly growing nonexistent cities." In Florida in 1925 you could invest in what the speculator thought was a con, a fraud, a scam, an outrageous and out-and-out inexcusable hustle—and still make money.

In such an atmosphere (as Roger Olien and Diana Davids Olien note in their study *Easy Money*), settling for 3 percent seemed downright unconstitutional. Returns of 100 or 1,000 percent were common, and any American could and should be rich. All you had to do was take the chance. Calvin Coolidge said, "Brains are wealth and wealth is the chief aim of man," less a presidential line than one that might have been uttered by an Elizabethan sharper from the pages of Robert Greene.

In the Midwest there was no land boom. Farmers and small businessmen who found themselves sitting on more spare cash than they'd ever had saw the advertisements in *The Saturday Evening Post* that said, "Do you sincerely want to be rich?" and wondered where to put their money. They didn't trust the great gambling casino of downtown Manhattan. To them it looked like a big-city operation, tricky and rigged. Stock swindles were so common that even Al Capone said, "It's a racket. Those stock market guys are crooked." So the Drake Estate didn't seem outlandish to them at all. Rather it seemed like a reasonable speculative possibility, not a sure thing, but with the chance of a spectacular return—a better bet than anything else. It became their own insider deal, talked of at picnics, at church socials, at bridge parties, in bars, and on farms. In the early days of Hartzell's control it attracted some of the same members as the then resurgent Ku Klux Klan: not just hicks and rubes and drivers of secondhand Fords, but doctors, store owners, insurance salesmen, members of the respectable and semiprosperous white middle class who could happily envision themselves rich as Rockefeller. Word went mouth to mouth. Hartzell's letters were passed around in secret and with great ceremony and an air of obfuscating mystery. A cult was called into being. Are you in on the deal? Come in on the deal. You have to be in on the deal.

A State Department official who traveled through the Midwest wrote:

> News articles concerning Hartzell and his agents would not be particularly interesting in the East beyond amusement over the fantastic claims of the "Baron," but in most states west of the Mississippi River the question is a vital issue and every article on the subject is read with interest and eagerness. Contrary to what I had supposed, contributors are not confined to ignorant persons and fools but there are thousands of otherwise normal citizens in Iowa, South Dakota, Nebraska, Kansas, Missouri, Texas, and elsewhere, who firmly believe they will share in an estate which is conservatively estimated at $22.5 billion but which is often represented as having a far greater value which surpasses the flights of imagination of all but the initiated.

This was prairie populism, a classic example of Main Street versus Wall Street. Especially in Iowa and Minnesota, the Drake Estate became a craze which split entire towns into believers and nonbelievers. Thousands put into the scheme every dollar they could get. Business suffered because people weren't paying their bills, and there was violence.

"I was working as a hired hand for a farmer," recalled an old-timer from Adrian, a small farming town on the southern Minnesota prairie. "One day my boss couldn't find me. He finally heard a ruckus out back behind the barn. Some of the local fellas were roughing me up, thinking that a working bachelor like me would have some extra money handy to buy some Drake bonds."

Father Otto Zachmann, the Catholic pastor of Adrian, reckoned that 90 percent of all the people in the surrounding countryside were donating every dollar they could rake and scrape to the Drake fund. From his pulpit he warned his parishioners to get back to honest work and not sit waiting for the impossible dream to come true.

"The fever of it is spreading like a plague and breaking down our people," Zachmann said. "They neglect their work and get together in groups and talk about the time, soon coming, when all of them will be millionaires. They have been promised $7,000 for each dollar they donate to the fund, and the old and the young are digging into their savings and investing all they have."

It was no use. People in Adrian, inspired by the dazzling hope of immediate wealth, went on giving all they had until at last Father Zachmann, tired of trying to warn them, left town.

FOUR

The Hunt

The first serious government attempt to stop Hartzell was made in 1928 by Ed M. Smith, Iowa's youthful and energetic secretary of state.

The Iowa Securities Commission had been denouncing the Drake Estate as a hoax since Sudie Whittaker's fateful appearance in Des Moines in 1915, and for years congressmen throughout the West appealed to Washington, saying they'd had complaints from their voters and were at a loss how to proceed, but Ed Smith was the first prominent official to see ending the swindle as part of his political mission.

Smith obtained and circulated a statement from the British consul general in Chicago that was clearer and more definitive than any issued thus far. The letter began with the usual assertion that "there is not, and has never been, any unclaimed Drake Estate." But it went on: "While there is nothing impossible in the contention that there may be some person living in America who is entitled to the Drake Baronetcy, it can safely be said that, having regard to the English law of landed property and inheritance, it is in the highest degree improbable that the establishment of a valid claim to the baronetcy could in any way affect the title of the present holder of the Buckland Abbey estate or any other property which may have belonged to the Drake family."

This tackled Hartzell in a direct way, spotting the confusion that he (and Whittaker and Lewis before him) had driven a truck through, the difference between running after an "unclaimed estate" and trying to get an estate that definitely did exist out of the hands of the people who owned it. It was now made clear that neither approach would work: no action in the British courts with regard to the Drake Estate was going to result in any money or property finding its way into the hands of Colonel Drexel Drake or Oscar Hartzell or anyone else.

The letter concluded: "I am authorised to say that all the activities which may take place in the United States in connection with the alleged Sir Francis Drake Estate can be assumed to be fraudulent and that the claim of Oscar Hartzell to a knighthood and a baronetcy is without foundation."

The document seemed definitive, and Ed Smith had it published in the Iowa and Minnesota newspapers, some of which, aiming to be fair, wishing to hear—as it were—from both the plaintiff and the defendant, ran answers from the Drake Estate promoters the following week. But Smith wasn't finished yet. Again showing how closely he'd studied Hartzell's particular version of the swindle, he introduced into the Iowa state legislature a bill which would require a permit "for the solicitation of certain donations" and would deny the granting of such a permit for any scheme deemed fraudulent.

If Smith barred Hartzell and his agents from accepting donations, the scheme really would be shut down. Hartzell cockily wired him from London: "You are making a damn fool of yourself, using your position and office to intimidate my donators. Before you go any further you had best get in touch with the authorities in Washington, who will tell you that everything is regular."

Charles Cochran struck off thousands of copies of this wire and circulated them among the Drake faithful. Soon every congressman and state representative in Iowa was bombarded with letters protesting what Ed Smith was doing, and when the bill came before the Iowa legislature the names of Washington and Jefferson were invoked, along with the idea that an American should be free to "do-nate" his money wherever he or she pleased.

Smith's bill was defeated, and he never tried to get it passed again; indeed, he didn't seek reelection as secretary of state, and soon retired from public office, his mission having ended in disappointing and puzzling failure.

Hartzell crowed: "Authorities here have notified Washington that I am OK. If I am a fraud, why don't authorities stop me? I advise you to act with great caution as your statements interfere in this matter and may work great hardship to the poor and faithful donators."

When the news was broadcast, people saw that these were indeed valid questions: if the estate was a fraud, why didn't Scotland Yard arrest Hartzell, why wasn't Washington stamping down on the scheme? Hartzell must be right or they would stop him. Money poured in.

A reporter from the *Kansas City Star* who went to see Dr. Charles Cochran at this time found a "large-bodied, middle-aged man" living in a comfortable and neatly built bungalow. In his office, stuffed into boxes, were all the papers relating to the Drake Estate and his receipts for the hundreds of thousands of dollars he was cabling to Hartzell. Cochran was in his shirtsleeves and wore a hat pushed back from his forehead. He spoke slowly and earnestly but in a very friendly way, emphasizing his points with little taps on the table with his pencil, reducing the combative newsman to puzzlement and finally exasperation. Cochran believed in Hartzell completely, he said, because he'd known him since he was a striving young farmer in Iowa. He knew all about the various statements that had been made by the State Department, and by the American embassy in London, and the British embassies in America, but he took Hartzell's word over theirs.

"The king and Parliament are afraid to let the people of England know about this deal," he said. "They're afraid that if the people knew all this gold was coming to America there would be a revolution. So they are selling off the docks and shipyards and towns on the Drake Estate in Devon, and all the buildings on this eighty-acre estate in the heart of London, so the people there won't get onto it until after the money is safe in America."

He agreed that, yes, there had been many unfortunate postponements, but Hartzell always had a good reason.

"They were just about ready to pay last year when the king of England took sick and that delayed it."

What had the king to do with it?

"Why, man, he had everything to do with it! The king had to go over it all, and he worked day and night, and worried over so much gold leaving the country and what the people would say when they found it out and it just naturally got him down. Hartzell cabled me all about it."

Hartzell had on this occasion needed an extra $6,000 (i.e., $60,000) at once, he said, so he sent the $6,000.

"Haven't you read where boatloads of gold have been coming to this country from England? That it was all taken and deposited for safekeeping in banks in New York? The papers said that it was England's part payment of her war debt to us. But that's just a stall. It was the gradual secret payment to Hartzell of a small part of the Drake Estate."

Hartzell said that?

"Hartzell knows," Dr. Charles Cochran said. Hartzell had been closeted with King George V, scheming a settlement of the deal; Cochran also believed that large blocks in the heart of London were being sold off and that many thousands of people in Iowa would soon be millionaires. He believed these things absolutely, he told the reporter from the *Kansas City Star*.

Reading this interview, I got the impression of a homely, practical, and straightforward man; either that, or a remarkable flimflam merchant indeed, entirely comfortable with his front as a down-to-earth country doctor. I think that Cochran was on the level, and the *Kansas City Star* reporter thought so too. Cochran's words went out, another solid layer of evidence around the fictitious entity of the Drake Estate. Radio stations picked up the story and ran with it, still without the scheme being discredited, and so those who believed were encouraged to go on believing, and in increasing numbers. The media packed weight and momentum around a snowball with a wisp of nothing at its core.

In Lima, Oklahoma, a sixty-eight-year-old autoworker who had never left Oklahoma and had never been given a day off work with pay in his life was asked what he would do when he came into his Drake millions.

"We shall give a share of the fortune to each of our children, so that they would never want for anything. We don't want to be estranged from them," he said. "Then of course we shall go to Europe and see the castles."

In October 1929 the bottom fell out of the New York stock market. The boom was over and the Depression began. Hopes were dashed, families ruined. Crowds of the distressed and curious stood around dead banks. We know the story, and much worse was to come: bankruptcies, unemployment, shantytowns, breadlines. In Iowa, grain and corn became much cheaper than coal and were burned to heat federal buildings, while those who could not keep themselves warm tore the seat covers off their cars and stitched them up into coats.

No such hard times for Oscar Hartzell: in October 1929 he hired himself a personal secretary, a retired British army captain named W. J. Stewart. Hartzell called him "my valet, one of the Royal Stewarts who once held the throne of Scotland." Perhaps he was remembering how Milo Lewis had scorned him all those years before. He wanted to make the point that now he had almost-royalty keeping his books and taking his suits to the cleaner. He paid Stewart £5 a week, not bad money in those days.

The crash put an end to most of the swindles that had characterized the decade, but not to the Drake Estate. Quite the reverse: the donors saw all their worst fears about Wall Street confirmed, and their faith in Hartzell grew only greater. "They now believe in Hartzell with the fire of the most rabid religious fanatics," wrote a State Department observer. As the Depression took hold and deepened, there was the bizarre and tragic spectacle of thousands of hard-struck people throughout the Midwest impoverishing themselves still further so they could send more and more money to Hartzell in London. They scraped, they borrowed, they mortgaged their houses and farms. What had begun as a speculation turned into a holy cause.

Oscar Hartzell was no longer merely in his pomp; he had become a champion of the people, and it paid like Hollywood. American Express records show that in November 1929, Dr. Charles Cochran wired him about $6,000 (more than $60,000 in today's terms); the following month it was $9,000 ($90,000); and in September 1930, $10,500. And the doughty Captain Stewart's ledger recorded that in the period June 1931–December 1932, Hartzell received more than $250,000 (i.e., more than $2.5 million) from America—a bewildering amount of money.

For Hartzell the crash was no disaster but a boon, each hour bringing fresh details, new contingencies he could weave into his never-ending story of delay. There was endless material for the misrule. News of the impending transfer of the fortune had leaked out and caused the crash, he said. Now the American money lords had ganged up with British financial interests and were fighting tooth and claw to prevent release of a settlement so vast and complex it would wreck the Bank of England and further rock the economic structure of the world. "We will see the hardest times in history before the estate is settled," he predicted. "And only then will things begin to get better."

On October 11, 1930, in *The Saturday Evening Post*, John Maynard Keynes published an essay attacking economic gloom and boosting the virtues of capital investment, even in difficult times. The essay, entitled "Economic Possibilities for Our Grandchildren," made reference to Sir Francis Drake and the treasure he stole from Spain. Keynes linked England's emergence as a world power directly to the good use Queen Elizabeth made of this money. She invested it, and arranged for England to take half the interest each year while the rest accumulated at a compound rate. "The power of compound interest over 300 years is such as to stagger the imagination," Keynes wrote. "Every pound which Queen Elizabeth invested in foreign trade has now become 100,000 pounds."

Keynes's point was that governments could spend their way out of depression, but Hartzell seized on the essay. Here was John Maynard Keynes, the world's top money man, echoing what he'd been saying all along: Sir Francis Drake! Compound interest! Staggering returns! Scores of thousands of mimeographed copies were distributed at Drake Estate booster meetings and throughout the Midwest. Puzzled government men found farmers in bib overalls spouting the theories of John Maynard Keynes. It was as if Keynes had endorsed the whole deal, and in the pages of *The Saturday Evening Post*, the revered journalistic bible of small-town America.

Hartzell was treated with yet more importance. He wasn't just their redeemer who was striving to bring home a fortune. He was an economic guru.

"You can see that the matter is so far reaching that the rambling minds of your great financiers of the past have been made to toe my mark regardless of consequence," he wired.

Questions came from South Dakota: "Does abandonment of gold standard affect your matter? Can you give us any definite idea of the close?"

He replied: "Cable received today as sent. Thanks. Matters moving very fast. All late important movements working for the good of the cause which makes the finish very close. Hartzell."

If questions pressed too hard, he replied in a vague way, writing darkly of "the powers that be" and "*the hidden hand*" (a concept he'd picked up from the writings of another famous economist, Adam Smith, maybe the only other one he knew about), mysteries he said he could not discuss without committing high treason. When there were grumblings from some of the Iowa flock, he immediately went on the attack, accusing them of being double-crossing jealous fools, trying to turn themselves into "the great I am." They would be kicked out, red-inked if they dared dispute any further. "There is only one great I am in this matter. His name is Oscar Hartzell," he wrote. If they wanted to look for someone to criticize, they should turn their direction elsewhere, to the corrupt politicians who were trying to queer their deal: "Pour the letters into Washington like pouring buckshot into a chicken thief. I would not trust one of the whole bunch down east in my chicken house in broad daylight. They are in a nice mess as I told you they would not be now if they had listened to me."

The psychoanalyst Phyllis Greenacre, who made a specialty of studying impostors and their mental makeup, wrote: "The impostor becomes temporarily convinced of the rightness of his assumed character in proportion to the amount of attention he is able to gain from it."

Oscar Hartzell was getting a lot of attention. He belabored and promised and defamed. He mixed belligerent imputation with rhapsodic promises. When he went into the offices of American Express on the Haymarket he was like a cyclonic disturbance, and his communications from this time give a powerful sense of the intoxication with which they were written. The whiff of mania was in his nostrils.

"I have a chain around the neck of every official who has ever crossed my path on either side of the Atlantic," he wrote. And the "great I am" was going to make them pay, from the highest to the lowest.

⌒

He got more, he spent more, loads of money: on cars, on clothes, on cigars, on women. If he was at dinner, at the Savoy or the Carlton, and someone wanted champagne, he would always call for a couple of bottles. He was supporting Eunice Colliss and his illegitimate son; he was transferring large sums back to America to his sister, Pearl, for herself and her family. And he was making himself conspicuous—things were getting out of hand.

Scotland Yard received an anonymous tip, unsigned, written carefully on a postcard in black ink: "The bulk of the money coming from the U.S. re Drake Affair is passed over to the woman as under—Mrs. L. B. Smith, 27 Elvaston Place, S.W.7."

Elvaston Place was a good address, in Kensington, and Sergeant

George Page, the detective who'd trailed Hartzell earlier, was sent over. He found "a painted lady, living in apparent luxury, surrounded by many soft cushions, canaries of variegated colors, and dogs of various breeds." Smith told Page she'd met Hartzell at Ascot, where he'd spoken casually of owning ranches himself and being a stock breeder. He'd told her he owned a gold mine, and since then they'd been seeing quite a lot of each other. Smith anxiously assured Page there was nothing intimate or improper in her relations with Hartzell, but Page gained the contrary impression. After the interview he waited in the shadows outside Smith's residence. "I saw Hartzell call and remain until after I had left," he wrote in his report.

It was true, in a way, about the gold mine—but Hartzell was growing careless.

Another letter came to the Yard, this one from A. R. MacGillicuddy, who had met Hartzell at a Tank Corps dance at Bobbington in Dorset. Charmed by Hartzell, MacGillicuddy and his wife had invited him to their home in Bournemouth for the weekend. They all had a good time, but something about Hartzell had so struck MacGillicuddy that he was impelled to write about it. "He mentioned that he was connected with the Sir Francis Drake Estate but did not approach me in connection with any financial transaction," he said. "Hartzell gave the impression that he was a man of wealth. But there was something suspicious about him, something strained and not quite right."

This visit to the MacGillicuddys' had one further important ramification. On his way back from Bournemouth, Hartzell ran his car into a ditch, was thrown out, and flew twenty-five feet over an embankment. Yet he rose to his feet with nothing more than bruises. He took this to be almost a miracle. While his American donors waited eagerly for his latest wire, studying the newspapers for any sign or hint of a settlement, he himself became superstitious. He started seeing a psychic.

Her name was Mrs. St. John Montague, and her rooms, in a house off the Fulham Road in South Kensington, were kept dimly lit at all hours. The atmosphere was heavy with the smell of incense; stuffed snakes and other reptiles were in glass cases on heavy oak tables; Pre-Raphaelite pictures of angels and demons and naked figures encoiled by serpents hung on the walls. Nina St. John Montague put on a good show, catering to the carriage trade, the smart set. She, like Hartzell, was doing well, for a vogue for what the novelist Anthony Powell called "the grisly vistas of the great beyond" persisted in London through most of the 1920s and into the Depression. Mrs. St. John Montague offered private meetings during the day, when she consulted the tarot pack or a crystal ball, and at night the promise of group communication with the afterlife over a ouija board. Hartzell went for one-on-one consultations. He told her he could easily afford it. He said he had a ship of gold, anchored out in the Thames.

The various published accounts of Hartzell's dealings with Mrs. St. John Montague derive from the same one source, Thomas Barnard, a witness who gave testimony at the Sioux City trial in 1933. Still, this episode has been presented in different ways. Karl Baarslag, a *Saturday Evening Post* reporter who studied the case in the 1930s and had access to federal investigators, wrote: "Hartzell had become infatuated with the clairvoyant's assistant, merely described as 'a dark-haired, Oriental charmer.'" Chicago journalist W. T. Brannon, who revisited the affair for *Mercury Book Magazine* in 1955 (and on whose story Jay Robert Nash seems to have relied in *Hustlers and Con Men*), picked up this detail and spun it a little further: Mrs. St. John Montague had "an assistant, a buxom dark-haired young woman who quickly caught Hartzell's eye. The clair-voyant told the girl to encourage the American to come back."

Thomas Barnard's deposition and court testimony make no mention of this "buxom dark-haired young woman," however, and nor does an excellent 1937 essay in the *Michigan Alumnus Quarterly Review* by Arthur Lyons Cross, a professor of English history and literature who also gave evidence at the 1933 trial and who spoke with Barnard a number of times.

The young temptress may be a gloss, an invention of Karl Baarslag, a knowing newsman who figured that beautiful and guileful women needed to be introduced into stories about confidence men, or indeed into any story at all, wherever possible. Or she may be quite real. We'll never know. Such are the difficulties of history.

All the sources agree on what happened next, however.

A few days after consulting with Nina St. John Montague for the first time, on January 7, 1930, at lunchtime, Hartzell was drinking in the American Bar at the Savoy when he fell into conversation with another American who happened to be there, a Texan as it turned out, an oilman on vacation. Hartzell, already drunk, was eager to talk, and reminisced about what he now thought of as the happiest and best days of his life, when he'd been partners with the great Robert Moody and had owned a big spread in the Texas panhandle.

The two men struck up such a rapport that when the Savoy Bar closed at three in the afternoon they shared a cab back to Hartzell's apartment on Basil Street so they could resume drinking. The friendly Texan had a confession to make. He said that the side of the oil business he'd been involved with hadn't been quite the honest side; it had been more of a stock promotion scheme. He was ashamed to say so, but he was in fact a bit of a confidence trickster.

One wonders what went through Hartzell's mind when he heard this. Was he suspicious? Did he laugh? Or was he so drunk that his usual instincts were obliterated and he almost clutched the Texan's shoulders and sobbed with relief?

He said that he too had once been involved with a bunch of crooks, chief among them a woman named Sudie Whittaker. It had been when he first came to England. He'd been mixed up with these people for a while, he said, before he realized they were working a con game. Since then he'd been working solely on the Drake Estate. There were thousands of claimants, and the estate was worth billions, he said.

"That sounds like a skin game too," the Texan said. "It's a wonder the authorities don't get after you."

Hartzell replied that the U.S. federal people had indeed been after him once but he had gotten away with it. He added that he was afraid of British lawyers, who were sharper than their American counterparts, he thought, and that he was being blackmailed by a Scotland Yard detective named George V. Page who was conducting a vendetta against him.

The Texan asked why.

Because of the Drake scheme, Hartzell said. "It is, of course, merely a racket, but based on an old legend. There are eleven hundred acres in the center of London that were part of the Drake Estate that have proved very attractive to my donators."

Remember that Hartzell must have been extremely drunk by now. He was exhausted by his masquerade, or merely trying to top his new pal; or maybe, nostalgic for the solid sense of self-worth he'd briefly enjoyed as a Texas rancher, he regretted what he'd become. For a few moments he seemed to be tired of putting something over on everybody and reverted to a less demanding role. He stepped out of the limelight and betrayed himself.

He said, "I am making money out of it, but I can't say that they will."

The mask slipped for only a few seconds, but Hartzell would be called to remember, for the Texan was in fact Thomas William Barnard, who later gave evidence in Sioux City. An Englishman, Barnard had once worked for the cotton merchants Merrifield Ziegler & Co. in Dallas. Hence he could do a convincing Texas accent. But in 1930 he was no longer in the cotton trade. He was the Barnard in Barnard & Howarth, Detective Agency, Swan House, Oxford Street, W1. Thomas Barnard was a private eye, hired by Nina St. John Montague to find out what he could about the wealthy Oscar Hartzell. Throughout the drinking session at Basil Street he kept asking to use the toilet, where he scribbled notes.

Barnard reported back to Mrs. St. John Montague, and the next time Hartzell went to see her she gazed into her crystal ball and saw uncannily accurate information about the Sir Francis Drake Estate and the past life and future career of Oscar Merrill Hartzell. Whether or not there was an alluring assistant involved, Hartzell visited Mrs. St. John Montague again and again, and was always astonished by her wisdom and insight.

The con man was handsomely clipped.

In the end the U.S. State Department, the FBI, Scotland Yard, and the U.S. Post Office Department each had files inches thick (in some cases several feet thick) on Oscar Hartzell and the Sir Francis Drake Estate. Reading through thousands of pages of documentation I came to realize not only just how very shrewd Hartzell had been to stay in London, committing no crime there while money gushed to him from America, but how difficult it had been for the various involved agencies to figure out exactly what he was up to, even before they could begin to try to do something about it. And when they did try they soon saw that Hartzell had left little or no direct evidence to incriminate himself. The swindle was on its face absurd and yet absurdly difficult to disprove—hence its genius. Letters and wires sped to and fro between detectives at Scotland Yard and diplomats in London and Washington bureaucrats. People put in charge of the case came and went, the buck was passed, or ignored altogether, and the cycle of paper shuffling would begin again. H. L. Stimson, the secretary of state in Washington, was asked the same question by scores of victims of the scheme, by congressmen, by senators, even (eventually) by the office of President Hoover himself: why was nothing done to prosecute Oscar Hartzell?

That this happened at all was in the end due largely to the work of one man.

John Sparks was another Westerner. He and Hartzell seem like brothers or doppelgängers, opposites in some ways similar. At six feet two inches and 235 pounds, Sparks was taller and even burlier, but he was of the same almost squarish build that made him appear constricted and slightly baffled in the suits he habitually wore. He looked as if he should have been out somewhere on a horse with a cowboy hat on his head. He had brown eyes and dark hair, cut short, graying at the temples. He was born in 1886 in Concordia, Missouri, a small community of prim white homes that had peony, rose, and dahlia gardens in front, and neat orchards and vegetable plots in the rear. His father taught at the local public school, and he was brought up in the strict, almost fundamentalist discipline of the German Lutheran Church, Missouri synod. As a teenager he played baseball, and was surprisingly swift and neat in his movements. Apart from stints in the military, he worked for the U.S. Post Office all his life. In 1931 he was married with children and had a strong sense of family and duty and order. He was an upstanding and clean-cut gentleman whose job was to protect the U.S. mails, and he had little sympathy with those who tried to get around the law. He was the man who was going to bring Oscar Hartzell to book.

The Post Office Inspection Service is the oldest and least-sung of the U.S. federal government's secret service agencies, even though more than 90 percent of the cases it brings to trial result in convictions. Post Office inspectors carry guns and sometimes go after mobsters and bombers, but their main target is fraud. Historically, in the same way that the charge of income tax evasion has been useful in the prosecution of the Mafia, con men are prosecuted more often than not under the wide-reaching federal statutes governing misuse of the mails. A con man might not use the mails himself, but if his scheme causes someone to write a letter, then the inspectors can take the case. Even today, in the era of FedEx and the Internet, it's not easy to commit systematic fraud without somewhere a stamp being licked.

As was customary, John Sparks worked for the Post Office for five years before he was allowed to take the inspectors' exam. After that, he apprenticed for a further year under an experienced instructor; then, based in St. Louis, he was thrown more and more on his own resources. Cases he investigated involved post-office stickups, burglaries, theft by employees, forgery of money orders and stamps, pornography, extortion, and the mailing of poisoned cakes and candies. Fraud, or "F," cases were at that time divided into thirty-one subcategories, a list which gives a thumbnail review of the state of the art of the con circa 1930. There were land swindles, oil well swindles, fake dog pedigree swindles, bogus work-at-home schemes, and bogus literary agencies; there were fake diploma rackets, astrology rackets, and fake prize contests. There were marriage swindlers, turf tipsters, mail-order Romeos, and men who sold and failed to deliver strawberry plants or a wide variety of wild animals.

And there were the genealogical rackets.

For some time, at the offices of the Post Office inspector in St. Louis, there had been an awareness that something big was happening in Iowa and Minnesota and South Dakota. Sparks first went to Iowa to investigate in 1928. He found many Drake donors, but none were willing to testify. They clung with exuberant faith to their dream of the golden deal, or told him to mind his own business. At that time he couldn't come up with enough evidence to warrant the risk and expense of prosecution.

With the crash, however, the Drake swindle was brought into high relief by the fading away of so many of the other frauds, and Sparks asked to be assigned the case on a permanent basis. This time he and his family moved to Sioux City, and he intended to stay there until the scheme was stamped out.

Hartzell soon received a letter, addressed ℅ American Express in London.

Dear Sir

I am a farmer living near Alton, Iowa, and some of my farmer friends have asked me why I did not donate something to the Drake Estate, which is to be settled through you. I understand that the money donated would be paid back two or three times. I have some loose money, but did not feel like donating until I know more about it, so I thought I had better write you. Banks have been failing and I have some money stored away for the right kind of investments. Will you please write to me relative to the matter, so that I may know what to do. An early reply will be appreciated.

Respectfully yours, H. W. Jansen.

H. W. Jansen was a trusted friend of the Alton postmaster, and the letter, one of more than five thousand sent out by Sparks as he began to gather evidence, was a trap, seeking to provoke use of the mails in return. Hartzell, feeling the presence of the enemy, easily saw through the dodge and sent back a wire, advising Jansen to consult in person with one of his agents.

Sparks went to see various of Hartzell's relatives, including his former wife Daisy (now remarried to a businessman) who said she didn't care if she never heard from or saw Oscar again in her life. Daisy was bitter. With no help coming from Hartzell's family, Sparks set out to discover who his agents were, driving thousands of miles to and fro across the Midwest to every Drake rally and pep meeting he heard about. These usually happened in the community room of a town hall or library, or at the local Chamber of Commerce—there was nothing secret about the way they were arranged; everything was quite open and apparently aboveboard. In time Sparks identified most of these men, and he found their profile to be the same. They were farmers, doctors, bank officials, insurance men, owners of small businesses, mostly churchgoers and middle-aged family men, known and trusted within their communities, men with social capital on which they could draw—men like the man Hartzell himself had been. Harry Osborn had a soft-drinks parlor and poolroom in Hartley, Iowa. A. C. Berry had a real estate office in Mitchell, South Dakota. Herman Landes was a blacksmith in Mallard, Iowa. Otto G. Yant was a bookkeeper in Des Moines. And so on. There were about thirty of them.

One of the agents, John Carlson, a salesman, arranged to meet Sparks in a hotel in Boone, Iowa, where on the dresser Sparks saw a package, a bundle of letters and telegrams from Hartzell in London, the very evidence he needed. Carlson refused to let him inspect the package, and Sparks resisted the temptation just to take it.

In general, none of these men attempted to lie or disguise what he was up to. Each admitted that he was gathering money and sending it to Hartzell; each insisted that the deal was for real.

Dr. Charles Cochran had died, and in Laurens, Iowa, Sparks caught up with Hartzell's new leading agent and booster in America, a farmer named Amos Hartsock. A middle-aged man in dungarees, his skin burned by wind and sun, Hartsock was plowing corn when Sparks interviewed him. His speech was homespun, but he was brazen and indignant, berating Sparks for trying to trick his boss into using the mails. "Why be so darned underhand about it?" Hartsock asked, and admitted using the mails to solicit and receive money. He also said he personally had wired large sums to Hartzell, somewhere between $700,000 and $800,000, he thought. He denied skimming any off the top, saying he took only what was necessary to cover the wire transfers and traveling expenses.

Hartsock was quite open and defiant, and Sparks had to confess that he was puzzled. Wasn't Amos Hartsock afraid that the Post Office was about to come down on him?

"No, because the deal's on the level," Hartsock said. He even asked if Sparks thought that Hartzell was a fraud, and when Sparks said he *knew* Hartzell was one, Hartsock only took off his hat, wiped the sweat out of his eyes, and shook his head sadly, as if he were being forced to explain something to a child.

"This whole deal is safer than government bonds," he said. "I'll give you an affidavit if you want—the whole thing's safer than government bonds."

⌒

John Sparks gave evidence of his discoveries at a series of hearings before the solicitor for the Post Office Department in Washington in

January 1931. Most of Hartzell's known agents were summoned. Amos Hartsock was an absentee, although five of the others, including the bookkeeper named Otto G. Yant, acknowledged that the Drake Estate was a swindle but claimed they were innocent victims of it. Faced with fraud orders (meaning they would be barred from using the mails, and any letter sent to them would be returned to sender marked "Fraud"), these five signed affidavits agreeing to stop soliciting and receiving money. This was reported widely in the Iowa press, the credibility of the scheme took a blow, and donations fell off.

Hartzell reacted as though he'd been betrayed by his children. Calling this backsliding "miserable Yantism," he became ferocious and resorted to his traditional weapon, Western Union. He wired Amos Hartsock: "Yant double-crossed me in Washington and lied to me and squandered my money. He failed to carry out my orders and too easily got down on his knees before authority. He jeopardized innocent donators' money and tried to defeat me and make me a traitor. He must be punished."

This fiery and calculatedly unreasonable missile of a message prompted Hartsock to reply that he was ready to fight publicly and burn Yant and the rest through the press. Hartzell, who admired Hartsock's spirit, liked the sound of that. Together they determined that Yant must be humiliated, ostracized, crucified.

Rowdy meetings ensued in Iowa; there was fierce dissent among the Drakers, with Yant emerging the loser for having questioned the deal. Realizing that he'd been made the "official goat," Yant bowed again, not to Washington this time but to the almighty Oscar Hartzell. He asked to be forgiven. He begged, but Hartzell was unbending, so a group of donors got together and timorously sent a petition, repeating their "profound faith" and begging for Yant to be allowed back into the fold, lest an organization "which had been working so smoothly and which has been so carefully and continuously oiled" fall apart in only a few short weeks. The petitioners pointed out that John Sparks hadn't got what he wanted in Washington; after all, no constraining fraud orders had been issued. They argued that Otto Yant had acted in good faith and that the cause had been helped, rather than the reverse, "since apparently the matter has been dropped by those who desired the reckoning."

This petition was touching testament to the donors' gullibility and the depth of their faith. At the time even Hartzell saw the justice of it, or at least the reality, and, as had happened so often in the past, a crisis served to launch the scheme into a heightened new phase. The expression of doubt had been in some way necessary; and once that doubt had been aired, belief reasserted itself with revived vigor. Yant went back to work, doubling his efforts, and donations, after the brief dip, soared. Soon Hartzell was receiving $15,000 a month.

He and the Iowa faithful got one thing wrong, however. Those "who desired the reckoning" didn't drop the matter. It was at this moment that finally they all began to pull in the same direction. Hartzell hadn't counted on John Sparks's dogged nature or his abilities as an organizer. The net began to close as Sparks and the Post Office Department supplied the State Department with a steady stream of reports that were then used by the American embassy in London to press the British Home Office either to extradite or deport the con man.

This brought its own wrinkle. The extradition treaty between America and Britain had only just been ratified, and Albert Halstead, the American consul general, doubted the wisdom of making Hartzell the first test case: it would be too risky a move, he thought, seeing the argument that could easily be made in Hartzell's defense—after all, if this crook had been living in England for more than fifteen years, why had the United States waited until now to try to get him back? At the same time, deportation (which involved the simpler task of persuading the British that Hartzell was an "undesirable alien") carried its own risk, because the legal mechanism didn't involve sending the offender anywhere specific once he was put on a boat and made to bid farewell to the white cliffs of Dover—which meant Hartzell could go to France, if he wished, or Germany, or Belgium, or Spain, or anywhere else that would let him in, and the very idea of Hartzell's leaving London only to set up shop in some other European capital with an American Express office sent the State Department into an anxious spin, clearly evident in all the documentation. Secretary of State Stimson and his people were determined to nab Hartzell, and to make their move only when they were sure of success.

While the machinery of governments decided how their gears should grind, Hartzell's chiding and goading of the donors became almost hysterical. He exhorted them not to believe the lying press. He reminded them that they themselves had been responsible for these latest delays by presuming to cross him. He said that soon he would supersede Ford and Rockefeller as the world's richest man and the pickings would be sweet indeed for those who had been true; and those who had not been, he added ominously, would be red-inked from the settlement. Franklin Roosevelt's landslide victory over Hoover in November 1932 seemed likely to allow him to go on playing his game indefinitely. Here was another fountainhead of potential delay. First Roosevelt seemed to be in favor of the deal, Hartzell said; then he was against. If the president-elect was photographed wearing his battered Italian felt hat, the news was good; if not—donors, watch out. Everything became a sign, and Hartzell's boasts grew wilder, his stories more extravagant, his rallying cries tougher and more despotic: "Give them hell! Stand your ground!

Defy the officials! I am boss!" He was starting to behave less like Melville's protean riverboat sharper from *The Confidence Man* than like Ahab, bent on a mission of doom.

⌒

At Scotland Yard, Sergeant George V. Page had been taken off the case. No evidence exists to suggest this was connected with Hartzell's blackmail allegation. More likely, the move was indication of the new seriousness with which the Yard was being forced to take Hartzell. A top man, Chief Inspector Charles Wesley, was now in charge. On December 12, 1932, Wesley and another detective, Sergeant Arthur Bishop, called at the apartment in Basil Street. They went early in the morning, before Hartzell had left for American Express and his daily rounds. Wesley's brief was clear: to assess whether, in his view, Hartzell knew the Drake Estate to be a charade and whether, therefore, the Home Office should deport him. Hartzell didn't realize the full implication of what was happening, but sensed something big was up. The record of the interview in the Scotland Yard file makes electrifying reading, a verbal fencing match between two adroit and nimble opponents.

Wesley asked the questions, and Hartzell replied while Bishop made notes in shorthand. Wesley observed that Hartzell was dressed with natty elegance and looked rich: silk shirt, silk tie, tailored wool suit. Wesley started off by telling Hartzell of the complaints the Yard had been receiving from America.

"Several hundreds, I should say," Hartzell said with nonchalance. He lit up a cigar.

"Are you the heir?"

"No."

"Are you the supposed heir?"

"That I cannot divulge," Hartzell said. He was high-handed and obstructive throughout the interview, toying with the detectives; certainly he'd been around authority and the law enough by now not to be frightened.

"Where is the Drake Estate?"

"I cannot tell you offhand."

"You had time to find out."

"I know but I cannot divulge."

Wesley knew the workings of the scheme inside out. "On 15th of November last, Mr. Hartsock, one of your agents in America, addressed a large body of citizens at Winnebago and said that you had established the identity of the one person who was entitled to the whole of the Sir Francis Drake property. Who is that person?"

"I cannot divulge. I think you will get that at the Home Office."

"Is it you?"

"No. I have the assignment of the heritage from the proper man whose name I cannot divulge."

"Have you ever seen the person?"

"No," Hartzell said, a chink in his armor, for he'd claimed to have met Colonel Drexel Drake on many occasions; but Colonel Drake was fiction, an invention, and he didn't want Wesley going in that direction.

"How do you know he exists?"

"From people who have done business for me."

"Who are these people?"

"I cannot divulge. It is a great mystery."

"You are getting plenty of money from this mystery."

Hartzell smiled and drew on his cigar. "Certainly I am," he said.

Wesley was demanding concrete evidence, and Hartzell had nothing to show: no worked-up genealogies, no letters, no affidavits, none of the documentation, albeit bogus documentation, with which

Whittaker and Lewis had defended themselves. He relied on arrogance, cheek, and bluster.

"I do not give a damn for all the officials," he said. "The American government has treated me very badly and I have no use for Americans or America. The American government has done some mean things, including interfering with my mail."

Hartzell finally said: "I am practically British. Someone at the Home Office arranged this for me and when all this is ended my name will suddenly become Drake and I will be a British subject."

With this astonishing statement the interview closed, and Hartzell was left guessing what might happen next. At this point there was no one he could turn to for advice. His friend Arthur Welch, like Dr. Charles Cochran, had passed on, and Hartzell had been the sole mourner when he was put in the ground at a cemetery in West London. Hartzell had liked Welch, and missed him.

On New Year's Eve, December 31, 1932, he dined at the Savoy Hotel, sitting as usual at his favorite table, number 101. In general in his autobiography he shies away from the subject of his later years in London, but something happened on this night that he had to describe. The incident involved Andrew Mellon, no less, then American ambassador to London, previously Hoover's secretary of the treasury.

"Andrew Mellon and his daughter got a table about 20 feet from mine. He got the information from the head waiter about which was my table and ordered his so he could face me directly. He wanted a table so he could get a good view of me. The head waiter said, 'Andrew Mellon must be interested in you.' Mellon stared at me for a long time."

The strangest thing about this piece of writing is its probable accuracy. Hartzell, at that moment, was very much on the mind of officials at the American embassy; it's certain that Mellon knew of the case and quite likely indeed that he would have been curious to take a good look at this rogue who was causing so much work and trouble. For once Hartzell was indeed close to a god of finance.

A few days later, Joy Broadburn came to see him for the last time. No doubt she wanted to get her money and jewels back, but something of the old affection still existed. She was worried about him. If he was deported, his donors in America would surely lynch him, she thought.

"I daresay they would if they could get hold of me, but I shall not go back," Hartzell said. He worked hard to persuade her of his invincibility. In the same way that, in his fantasy, every powerful American was his mortal enemy, he tried to convince her that the entire British establishment was lining up on his side. He claimed to be receiving help from one of the oldest and richest families in England, the Cecils, whose most illustrious ancestor had known Sir Francis Drake and had been Queen Elizabeth's trusted adviser. "They've sold their family portraits to assist me," he said.

He assured Joy Broadburn that one day they would live in Blenheim Palace (the country seat of the Churchills, not the Cecils, but Hartzell wasn't worrying about details) and also that most of Oxford was his, although they must have a small place first.

"Everything will be all right," he told her.

On January 9, Sergeant Arthur Bishop came back to Basil Street, this time with another detective, Inspector Chapman, who told Hartzell that the Home Office had issued a deportation order against him and he was under arrest. Hartzell was so shocked and enraged that for a moment he tried to resist. The two detectives subdued and handcuffed him, and he was hurried to a waiting police car. As the car sped away, Chapman handed him a copy of the deportation order.

"They won't deport me. I can easily straighten this matter out," Hartzell said, recovering some of Baron Buckland's bullish bravado.

He was taken to Brixton police station, where he was evasive during questioning. It was discovered that he had about his person almost $5,000 in cash. The previous month, ironically, had been his most lucrative to date—he had received more than $18,000 (more than $180,000). He was allowed to order his meals in, and continued to eat and drink lavishly, even while incarcerated.

On the cold and foggy afternoon of January 31 he was bundled into another police car and driven into the center of town, to a building in Whitehall, where he was given his chance to speak before the Aliens Deportation Advisory Committee and appeal its decision. He made no attempt to do so; it didn't occur to him to ask whether he could go anywhere else except America when he left Britain.

"All I have to say is that I am ready to go," he said.

No official finesse was required. The State Department need not have worried. Hartzell was quite resigned at this point. He wanted to go home, and wrote to the Metropolitan Police commissioner, asking that a "first class ticket on as good a boat as possible" be bought from the money he had with him at the time of his arrest. He also asked to be taken back to his apartment so he could collect some clothes. "I don't want to inconvenience you any more than I can help," he wrote. "Would you please advise me as soon as possible what boat I will go on and when? It will be a great relief to know."

On February 8, two detectives drove him once more from Brixton into central London. He asked if he could take them to lunch, they agreed, and the three of them went to Simpson's-in-the-Strand, then as now one of the best restaurants in town. He drank, and smoked cigars, and the detectives motored him around for a couple of hours, generously letting him have a last look at the great city he'd grown to love. Hartzell collected his luggage from Basil Street and, quiescent, but under escort, was put on the boat train to the familiar town of Plymouth. He sailed the next morning, traveling in a first-class stateroom on the French Line's SS *Champlain*, the boat that seven years later would bring another sort of trickster, the writer Vladimir Nabokov, to America. The crossing was rough, and Hartzell, watching the mountainous walls of the Atlantic heave and fall around him, was journeying toward the most astounding events of his life.

FIVE

On Trial and on Top

The classic psychoanalytic study of the impostor was published in 1925 by Karl Abraham, an early follower of Sigmund Freud. Abraham's paper "The History of an Impostor in the Light of Psychoanalytic Knowledge" concerned the life history of a man, simply referred to as N, on whom he'd made a report when he'd been an Austrian army medical officer during World War I. N was a compulsive: imposturing was a neurosis with him. That's to say he would adopt an identity, shed it when discovery was imminent, and adopt another; sometimes he was clumsy, and allowed himself to be caught, but he was so adept at winning confidence that on these occasions he usually contrived to make his guards careless, "thereby allowing him to escape without the slightest violence."

N acted out of motives of self-aggrandizement; he wanted to be loved, to be rich and admired, and he never burned with a brighter flame than when he was pretending to be someone he wasn't. Rid of the inhibiting uniform of his own biography, he sparkled and triumphed, while sowing the self-destructive seeds that would soon bring disaster and the necessity of a new, yet more inventive, imposture. As a boy, like Dexter in F. Scott Fitzgerald's story "Winter Dreams," he always felt he was on the outside of the window, looking in; he didn't smash the window, or try to figure out a map or route that would enable him to reach the other, more desired side of the glass, the side where the glittering things were—he simply lied himself in. But that's far too blunt as a description, because N's lies were anything but simple; they were supple and subtle creations in which the urge of his own need flowed smoothly and even elegantly into the shapes desired by his victims. N identified with his victims so rapturously that he became them, and as soon as it looked as if the artifice was about to be ripped or cracked or undone, he vanished.

Impostors, confidence men, are, in a way, like artists, their creations being the false selves or phony constructs that they impose upon us, and N was a character whose cavortings would not have been out of place in Oscar Wilde's *The Importance of Being Earnest*, and whose life did, in fact, provide material for the later chapters of Thomas Mann's novel *Confessions of Felix Krull, Confidence Man*, in which Krull, out of his desire to rise in the world, impersonates a nobleman and successfully cons a king.

The attraction of N's story might be that most of us know, or at least sense, that our permanent identities can be a bore and a constraint we accept with reluctance. We dream of being in other places, other times, other skins. Given human fretfulness and restlessness, the attraction is universal, although those who act on the fantasy find that mixing up identities can produce a Molotov cocktail as easily as a martini. Joseph "Yellow Kid" Weil talked about the story of Colonel Jim Porter, a former Mississippi steamboat gambler. As part of a scheme, Weil introduced Porter to a number of people as "Colonel Porter, who owns an island in Florida," and then realized that pretty soon Porter was convinced he actually did own an island in Florida, and that those people who weren't in on the ruse believed every word he uttered. In his case the mask became the face. "Colonel Porter lived the part of the retired millionaire so well that in time he came to believe it," Weil wrote, with the scorn of one who always knew where he stood, even in relation to his own playacting. Colonel Porter was a very good con man, apart from the fact that he was mad.

In his book *The Adversary* the French writer Emmanuel Carrère told the hair-raising true story of Jean-Claude Romand, apparently a loving father and a successful doctor, who deceived and defrauded his family for eighteen long years and, when the lie of his life was about to be discovered, killed his wife, his two children, and his mother and his father before trying (and failing) to kill himself. This happened in 1993. Romand's entire mode of being was the lie, and one of the most chilling moments in the story is when he met attorneys and psychiatrists and, as Carrère notes, underestimating the problem of trying to leave a favorable impression after one has just slaughtered one's family, used the same techniques of performance that had worked so well in the past: a dignified composure, a solicitousness of others, a worldly calm. He was like a robot that didn't know it was broken. The psychiatrists' report concluded: "He will never, ever, manage to be perceived as authentic, and he himself fears that he will never know if he is. Before, people believed everything he said; now no one believes anything anymore and he doesn't know what to believe."

I mentioned earlier that my own father was a crook, a con man. Having served with the RAF during World War II, having had, as they say, a good war, he found himself restless and out of place in the dingy and depressed atmosphere of northern England in the years after 1945. He had a business, an undertaker's business, but it failed even though he always worked hard and was a charmer, a social success. People liked him because he was rakish and funny and generous and could be counted on to continue playing the part of the devil-may-care fellow who was never happier than with a woman at his side, a drink in one hand, and in the other the Parker fountain pen he employed to write checks that were almost certainly going to bounce. He was fun to be around, and all his life he was engaged in hide-and-seek with a severe depression, his "blacks" as he called them. I had a jolt when, reading Oscar Hartzell's prison file, I came across Daisy Hartzell's remark "My husband had many acquaintances, but no friends." That was my father exactly. No one ever got too close, and his charm as much as his temper was what kept them at arm's length.

He had a chip on his shoulder about the fact that of the two businesses that could have come to him through his father's side of the family, he'd got the one involving horses and coffins, rather than the other, the more obviously promising prospect, a farm in a far snootier part of the country than the one where he lived. Like Hartzell, he was always haunted by the Texas that might have been, by the fantasy of the rich and respectable life that could, if only things had gone the other way, have been his.

By 1969 he had another business, a car dealership, but it was in trouble. He'd taken delivery of a number of cars and had sold them, pocketing the money rather than sending it to the manufacturers. Now the dogs were closing in. He was overdrawn at the bank, he was drinking too much, and his business was the subject of gossip and speculation. I think he was very angry and frightened. One night, in his cups, he slapped my face so hard my head swiveled. Soon afterward, having taken delivery of yet more cars, and having sold them and grabbed the cash, he faked his own death and disappeared with a phony passport. He fetched up in South Africa, in the beautiful city of Durban, and he lived there for years under an assumed name. He had a job, a lover, possibly even a whole other family. We never discovered all the details.

Eventually, many years later, when I was a university student, my father came back to England and, with his then mistress, set himself up in the antique trade, still operating under a bogus identity. One day a policeman knocked on his door and said, "Hello, Jack," presenting my father with a choice that involved more than the mere telling of lies or truth. He confessed, was arrested, tried, sentenced; it was while he was in jail that I began to get to know him again.

He told me that while he'd been on the run, living under assumed names and with fake passports, he'd never forgotten about his family (my brother and sister and me) and had known that one day he would want to come back to see us. I think that was partly true, although I also think he was both fooling himself and playing me for a sap when he said it. I think he came back because he was exhausted by the performance and he knew returning was the only way he could become Jack Rayner again; so, in many ways, the appearance of that policeman at the door had been a relief, a blessing, a summons not just from the law but from his own self.

He died in 1992, and I still often wonder what he thought about when he was alone at night in pubs and hotels in various cities around the world. That's a persistent image I have of him: standing in front of a darkened window, or a mirrored bar, whiskey in hand, and catching sight of his own reflection for a second just before he turned away from it. In those later years he spoke of his experiences on the run but never asked himself how they'd acted on him, or others. Perhaps that particular guilt was too great for him to draw into himself and talk about in an authentic way. His attitude was bluffly: "It's all in the past now"—as though all the games, all the fraud, all the lies, all the imposture, all the cons both petty and great, had involved not him but some other character he'd been fortunate enough to escape. This good luck and fortunate piece of personality management became central to the way he viewed himself. He'd walked a narrow but dangerous road. He'd taken dreadful chances with his mental balance but survived. Like Odysseus, he'd traveled and returned, grasping his home and his identity before it shimmered away down the street in front of him.

"I've not done too bad," my father said many times. "I came back, didn't I?"

~

On February 15, 1933, the night that Giuseppe Zangara, a New Jersey bricklayer, fired six times at Franklin Roosevelt, missing him with all six shots but fatally wounding the unfortunate Anton Cermak, mayor of Chicago, the SS *Champlain* approached New York Harbor and stopped at quarantine, about ten miles out.

Next morning John Sparks rode on a motor launch into the bay. With him were O. B. Williamson, another postal inspector; Alvin Sylvester, an assistant U.S. attorney; and George J. Oetzel, a U.S. marshal from Sioux City, who was armed with a pistol and a warrant for Hartzell's arrest.

Sparks had been planning this surprise ever since hearing of the *Champlain*'s departure from London. Clad in a thick overcoat (it was a clear and bitterly cold morning in New York), and followed by the rest, he clambered aboard the *Champlain,* where he was met by Guy Ray, a vice-consul from the American embassy in London.

Ray had been keeping a secret eye on Hartzell throughout the voyage. Several times he had stood next to the swindler on deck or as he leaned against the rail, pondering the sky. He had espied him across the crystal and silverware in the sumptuous first-class dining room. A suave and ironic Southerner, from a small town in Alabama, Ray was a man who had come far and already seen much in his life, but he drew particular satisfaction and amusement from this cloak-and-dagger operation. Now he led Sparks and the rest toward Hartzell's quarters.

By the time they got there the party had grown. The captain of the ship had joined them, and various officers, all curious about the drama, and anxious that the reputation of the French Line not be undone by harassment of any of their passengers, especially a first-class one.

Sparks rapped on the door, and a sleepy Hartzell opened it.

"It was terrible," Hartzell said later. "There were forty or sixty of them." No doubt he exaggerated; but there was a posse.

Hartzell, given a few minutes to dress, was hauled off to the purser's office.

Sparks reached in his pocket and pulled out five letters. These letters, evidence he'd been seeking for years, had been seized in a raid on Amos Hartsock's house only a few days before. Sparks asked Hartzell to look the letters over and say whether he'd written and mailed them.

Hartzell examined each of the letters carefully, and said yes, he'd written and mailed them.

For Sparks this was important; in front of many witnesses, Hartzell had confessed to using the mails.

Now Sparks produced a sheaf of telegrams. Had Hartzell written these too?

Hartzell said it was hard to remember; in London he'd sent more than four thousand telegrams, he said.

Sparks asked where the Drake Estate was, and Hartzell waved his hands and said it was "all over." Sparks asked with which courts he'd taken up his claim.

"The Ecclesiastical Courts and the powers that be," Hartzell said automatically, reverting to one of his formulas.

U.S. attorney Alvin Sylvester chipped in. "How is the unclaimed Drake Estate coming along?"

Hartzell, who had been in a state of some agitation, smiled at this old mistake. "There is no such thing as an unclaimed Drake Estate."

Only now did U.S. marshal George Oetzel produce his warrant and tell Hartzell that he was going to be arrested.

Hartzell was astonished. He hadn't known what to expect on his return to New York. He hadn't allowed himself to think about what might happen. Certainly he hadn't imagined this: to be plucked from the security of his first-class stateroom and arrested in front of the crew on the *Champlain*. He was very shaken.

"That Post Office boy told a pack of lies about me about what happened on the boat," Hartzell claimed later, when he denied having admitted writing the letters. But I think we can trust John Sparks's version of these events. Hartzell's bitterness arose from his knowledge that on the *Champlain* he'd have been better advised to keep his mouth shut and demand a lawyer. Instead of which, taken aback, he talked. Sparks's plan worked.

After the *Champlain* docked, Sparks rushed Hartzell through customs and took him to Alvin Sylvester's office in the New York Federal Building for more questioning. Sparks read him Arthur Bishop's notes of the December 12 interview at Basil Street and asked if they were an accurate report.

Hartzell saw now that this was a forceful and well-orchestrated attack.

Next day, on February 17, the arrest was news in all the papers. The *New York Times* carried this item: "A mild-mannered man with ruddy cheeks, which owed their color, Federal Authorities reported, to high living in London cafés on the $800,000 he collected from victims in America, the prisoner Hartzell told Alvin Sylvester, Assistant United States Attorney, that everything 'is above board and I can prove it.' "

By then Hartzell was aboard trains, speeding west with Sparks and Oetzel to Chicago, then changing onto the Illinois Central bound for Iowa.

All the while, Sparks went on pressing him with questions. Hartzell was chatty and expansive when talking about Whittaker and

Lewis, and was even willing to discuss the roles of his various American agents, but was evasive when asked exactly what he'd been doing with his time and with the money, and Sparks's report of these conversations is filled with those same phrases we've heard so often: "cannot divulge," "the powers that be," "the hidden hand," "Ecclesiastical Courts."

Hartzell was gathering himself during those long hours with the tracks clicking beneath him and his homeland speeding by outside the window, and by the time the Illinois Central pulled into Sioux City, on a crisp Sunday morning with snow in the air, he was no longer the man who'd been in shock on the *Champlain*. He was quite composed. He'd begun to realize just what a big deal he was in America, and I believe he'd already decided what he was going to do.

Church bells were pealing as he stepped down from the train and saw scores of people at the entrance to the station beyond the barrier. They cheered as soon as they saw him, waving and shouting his name. Newspaper photographers rushed along the platform to capture the moment. He'd returned to America to find a crowd not wanting to lynch him, as Joy Broadburn had feared, but longing for him to be who he claimed to be. A crowd of hundreds who believed in him, in his deal, in his competence, in his ability to make them rich and save them.

John Sparks refused to have his picture taken alongside Hartzell, and so George Oetzel posed instead. Essentially the two men were dressed the same: shoes, topcoat, shirt and tie, hat. But the photographs taken that morning showed two very different men. Oetzel wore clumpy policeman's boots, while Hartzell sported polished brogues from Jermyn Street; Oetzel's fedora was pushed back on his head, while Hartzell's English bowler sat squarely above his eyes, and he stood square-shouldered and square-jawed; Oetzel's coat flapped about his knees and had seen better days, while Hartzell's was longer, and sumptuously cut. George Oetzel looked like a workingman, while Hartzell looked like confidence—he looked like money. He had with him his splendid steamship trunk, which, the *Sioux City Journal* reported, contained "10 tailored suits, 20 silk shirts, 10 pairs of shoes, 100 towels, several overcoats, and innumerable ties and handkerchiefs."

John Sparks hurried Hartzell through the crowd without letting him address them, but then it turned out that the cab driver who sped them away, first to Sparks's office, then to breakfast, and then on to the county jail, was a Hartzell supporter, a Drake donor who wouldn't stop talking and wouldn't accept a fare. It was an honor, he said, to ride with Oscar Hartzell.

Guy Ray, the State Department diplomat who'd shadowed Hartzell on the *Champlain*, arrived in Sioux City two days later to help prepare the indictment for the grand jury. Astonished by what he saw and heard throughout Iowa, he wrote:

> According to stories circulating here, and firmly believed by thousands, Consul General Halstead was fired from London because he interfered with Hartzell's activities. The same reason also accounts for the departure from London of Ambassador Dawes; a few will admit that Ambassador Mellon, being a Republican, probably resigned, but insist that he would have had to leave anyway. Newspaper clippings were shown me relating Lloyd George's recent threat to reveal the secrets of certain cabinet meetings and how the British Empire was rocked to its foundation. It was confidently believed that reference was made to the fear of the British Government that people would learn of the impending ruin of the country due to the imminent settlement of the Drake Estate. It is stated that when

President Roosevelt refers to open diplomacy he is endeavoring to have the British agree to the publication of the facts of the matter. Further, the gold embargo was necessary because the United States Government was responsible to Hartzell for the gold it had collected on his behalf from England. Hartzell and his agents have even claimed that the final settlement will include all the territory north of the Rio Grande and west of the Mississippi, the basis of the claim being that during his travels Sir Francis Drake landed in what is now California and laid claim to the region. The fact that none of Canada is claimed is cited as evidence of reason and moderation and proof that no territory is being claimed beyond that to which legal title can definitely be established.

In the Woodbury County jail, Hartzell treated his fellow inmates to cigars and cigarettes and candy. Five days after his arrival in Sioux City, on Friday, February 24, 1933, he was released on $10,000 bail. That night he met with more than a hundred of his supporters at the West Hotel. In one eyewitness account, Hartzell stood and addressed the meeting in ringing tones, demanding $15,000 to clear his debts and $2,500 a week for expenses, and promising that he would deliver the estate of Sir Francis Drake in full by June 1. In another telling, Hartzell—dressed in a dark blue overcoat, a black jacket, and striped gray trousers, looking once again like a plutocrat—sat silent and impressive, playing the part of the remote and revered leader, cloaking himself in mystery while others beseeched him to press on, complete the deal, show the world.

More than $68,000 was raised for his defense in the next few months. The June 1 deadline he'd set for himself came and went and no one complained. Local senators and congressmen were hounded by angry Drakers. At the offices of the *Sioux City Journal* and the

Sioux City Tribune the phones in the city room jangled and rocks sailed through the windows because those papers took an anti-Hartzell position.

In the long, hot, dry summer of 1933 there were boiling dust storms and plagues of grasshoppers and locusts across the plains. It was a dark, almost apocalyptic time. John Dillinger began to blaze his trail through the Midwest. But Sioux City had its own sensation, and Oscar Hartzell, his self-esteem fanned by teams of lawyers and frequent meetings with his loyal followers, realized there could be no question of confession or backing down. His mind became rigid and set. On his return to America he found himself feared and venerated, the leader of a mass popular movement. People were awed by him. He was a success beyond even his own extravagant dreams.

Like Odysseus, Oscar Hartzell had indeed returned, but he wasn't coming back; and Guy Ray, for one, believed that he would never be found guilty in the state of Iowa.

—

The trial of *United States of America* v. *Oscar M. Hartzell* opened at ten in the morning on Monday, October 23, 1933. It began slowly, as trials tend to do. Nonetheless there was the sense of a great battle about to be fought. All seats were filled in the Sioux City courtroom, and outside, in the corridors and lobbies of the federal building, eager onlookers pressed to get in. One farmer, disappointed, said: "This sort of thing ought to be pulled off in a stadium."

Prosecutor Harry Reed believed this the most important trial in Iowa in a generation, and yet the scene was less judicial than something out of P. T. Barnum. People harried and hassled Reed, branding him a Wall Street stooge and a lackey for the government. Then they raised their hats and cheered when they caught a glimpse of

Hartzell, the great leader, dressed in a pin-striped blue shirt and an expensive suit of sober gray, arriving with his lawyers. People surged forward, exhorting him to stick with it, win through, show the crooked authorities. It occurred to Reed that the entire state had been split in two by this affair. You were either in favor of Hartzell or against him, and the former were in a big majority. Reed later wrote:

> Hartzell's campaign had reached evangelistic proportions. It was like the crusades in the Middle Ages. One church fired the preacher because he opposed a contribution. If you did not believe in Oscar Hartzell, you better keep your mouth shut. I talked to hundreds of people who had contributed before, during, and after the trial and I never found anyone who did not think he had made a good investment.

Harry Reed was head of the American Legion and a member of the Library Board in his hometown, nearby Waterloo. He'd played on his college football team, had served as an artillery officer in World War I and would serve again, as a captain in USAF intelligence, during World War II. He was lean and tall and had a long narrow face with an oddly protuberant lower lip that was plump as a cushion. Reed was unflappable and bound by honor.

By way of contrast, Hartzell's defense was in the hands of the flamboyant Carlos Goltz. Born in Taylorsville, Kentucky, of Russian parents who owned a string of lumber mills, Goltz had arrived in Sioux City via the Chattanooga College of Law and the law school at the University of Dakota. He was one of the most successful and best-known lawyers in town, a ladies' man, a member of the Izaak Walton League of America, and an amateur (and published) Lincoln scholar. Already a figure of some wealth, he would nonetheless always arrange for his supplier of bootleg booze to be raided by the police so he could pay his large bills with legal services rather than cash. When he played golf foursomes at the local country club he insisted on a fifth caddy to carry the whiskey. "He drank and was an alcoholic and was darned good and it didn't seem to hurt him any. Carlos Goltz was plenty smart," an Iowa Supreme Court judge who remembered him well told me. Goltz looked oddly like a balding Mick Jagger.

Harry Reed and the other chief prosecutor, special attorney John S. Pratt, squared off against Goltz in front of Judge George Cromwell Scott, a former congressman appointed to the bench by Warren Harding in 1922. Scott (a relative, incidentally, of the actor George C. Scott) was thought to be firm and fair, and his rulings were almost never overturned. He had pure white hair, sharp features, and blue eyes that looked severe and authoritarian behind wire-rimmed spectacles, although his favored reading—Twain, Dickens, detective stories—suggested a puckish side to his character. A self-made man who'd worked for years as a farmhand, teaching himself law in the winter, he had little sympathy with business types gone to the bad.

Oscar Wilde said that all trials are trials for one's life, and here were the men who would decide Hartzell's.

To secure a conviction, Harry Reed and John Pratt had to satisfy the jury on three points: that Hartzell had used the mails; that money had changed hands as a result; that he had known the purpose for which money had been sought to be bogus and fraudulent.

John Sparks, the government's first witness, quickly took care of point number one, describing his interview with Hartzell on the *Champlain* and entering the crucial five letters as exhibits. In cross-examination, Goltz sought to impugn the strange and artificial circumstances of the *Champlain* meeting, but made no dent in Sparks's impressive testimony or his credibility.

A doctor, a Chamber of Commerce secretary, a washerwoman with seven children, and a blacksmith were among those next called, and here things went more Goltz's way. Each admitted donating money to the Drake scheme, but, although they were all witnesses for the government, each insisted that he or she believed in Oscar Hartzell completely. On the stand Amos Hartsock said, "Our deal is the cause of the depression, having tied up the finances of the whole world," and murmurs of agreement spread around the court, prompting Judge Scott to reach for his gavel.

Nonetheless Reed and Pratt were making their second point: Hartzell had solicited and received money.

The trial had been progressing for more than a week already, and in the press gallery the action thus far felt like mere sparring. These were tough Depression-era newsmen from Chicago, Toronto, Des Moines, and Cincinnati, reporters who were like ringside spectators at a prizefight. They wanted savage blows and drama, and when none seemed to be forthcoming they looked among themselves for amusement. A female reporter from the *Sioux City Tribune* became known as Maid Marion because her name was Marion and she changed the color of her dress and hat every day and was so beautiful bored eyes drifted magnetically in her direction. One newsman polled the jury: "Bald, 1; Hirsute, 11; Mustached, 1; Smooth-faced, 11; Bespectacled, 4; Unspectacled, 8. Later: one of the jurors has just donned dark glasses, making the count 5 to 7." They passed ribald notes between themselves or made bets, about the outcome of the trial, about when and where John Dillinger would be caught, about the color of Maid Marion's hat the next day, and about the identity of a mysterious government witness who had arrived and was keeping very quiet and had been identified by Harry Reed only as "Mr. X."

Who was this Mr. X?

Heads craned to get a better look at him, but no one knew.

Mr. X: the trial even had a secret agent.

In the tense atmosphere, laughs were few and seized upon.

J. W. Ferguson, a railroad engineer, seventy-one years old, was asked how much money he and his wife had invested in the scheme. He said they had each donated $1,000. "But I put one over on her and sneaked in an extra $175."

Hartzell himself joined in the giggle that swept through the court.

Reed and Pratt moved on to their third point, trying to prove that Hartzell had known the scheme to be fraudulent. To do this they had to introduce a lot of information about Sir Francis Drake, in order to show that what Hartzell had been saying was nonsense and pure invention. They called Dr. Arthur Lyon Cross, from the University of Michigan, author of *A Short History of England,* then a widely used textbook.

Cross's job here was a curious one: he was testifying about academically accepted history and seeking to establish that it was, in fact, fact. But as soon as he began to speak about how Drake had organized his privateering ventures, Carlos Goltz interrupted him.

"All history is inaccurate. All history is badly written," Goltz said.

This thrust, this spontaneous courtroom jab, revealed one of the ways in which Goltz was thinking about Hartzell's defense. It also pointed straight to the heart of an ambiguity and confusion on which the Drake Estate swindle was founded, the idea that when it comes to the past, none of us know what really happened.

If, as Goltz said, all history is inaccurate, it becomes possible not only to make up your own history but to engineer a situation where that version of the story becomes as widely believed as any of the official ones. Hartzell, unconsciously, or maybe not, had allowed his con to bubble out of these ontological quicksands; he relied on the ultimate unprovability of all history. The past is gone; we need evidence to re-create it, and the very plainest evidence can usually be interpreted in all sorts of ways. So who's to say that Drake didn't have an heir no one ever knew about? Who's to say he didn't have an affair with Queen Elizabeth? In 1933 the poet Robert Graves had just completed his first novel, *I, Claudius,* the putative autobiography of the fourth Roman emperor, Claudius. The device of the book, its literary stratagem, was the suggestion that this was the straight dope of Imperial Rome, the secret history of the murders, poisonings, and skulduggery that the official record dared not show. Likewise, Hartzell had reconfigured and rewritten history, had discovered that this worked dramatically, and Goltz, himself a historian (and one who evidently believed history fundamentally unreliable), saw that those revisions were now a part of the public consciousness in Iowa. And might they not be true? Weren't transactions of importance involving those like Sir Francis Drake very often wrapped in doubt and obscurity? Who was to say, in the end, that a professor from the University of Michigan was a more reliable historian than a onetime Iowa farmer who had really looked into his stuff?

Goltz, having noted the flash with which Hartzell dressed on arrival in Sioux City, told him to tone it down in court. So Hartzell did his best to appear merely solid and worthy, in a sober gray suit and a blue silk tie, although he couldn't stop fiddling with his many expensive pairs of glasses, and with the ruby ring that adorned his pinkie. It was the one that he'd taken from Joy Broadburn, or that she'd given him, many years ago. Further image control was attempted when he and Goltz went over to the press gallery and handed out a portrait that they'd had taken in a local studio.

"Now, boys," Hartzell said, "I wish you'd use this good photo of me." And it *was* a good photo: in it he appeared dignified, yet approachable, a businessman, affluent yet not swaggering. He liked it a lot better than another the papers had been running, taken in the New York customhouse when he was still dazed after his arrest on the *Champlain*. In that one he was striding toward the camera with an anxious smirk on his face and one of his trademark Perfecto cigars set at an angle in the corner of his mouth. In that one he looked like a confidence trickster.

At the end of each day's session, Hartzell lit his cigar and, surrounded by well-wishers, walked to the Martin Hotel, where he'd taken over an entire wing for himself and his closest associates. The government had sectioned off another wing for the jurors. Hartzell ate his meals on a raised dais at one end of the dining room. Supporters waited in the lobby for him to emerge, hoping to shake his hand or touch his coat. They watched him through the glass doors. Occasionally Hartzell made a sign and one of his lieutenants let in a lucky someone, who walked all the way across the room to exchange a few words with the great man.

For him the trial was only the latest in a long line of adversities, and he had no intention of hiding or skulking. He was where he liked to be, in the limelight, and he lorded it, defiant.

⁓

The case against him picked up speed.

Guy Ray, the State Department man, cleverly introduced a summary of the Scotland Yard interview at Hartzell's home—Goltz had this part of the testimony stricken as hearsay, but not before the jury had heard it. Dr. C. Percy Powell, an Elizabethan scholar from the Manuscripts Division of the Library of Congress, caused a sensation by producing in evidence a photostat of the last will and testament of Sir Francis Drake, at that time the oldest document ever presented in an American court, having been filed for probate more than 330 years before. "In the name of God, Amen," the will began. In it Drake remembered his wife, his brothers, his creditors, his servants, even a servant of his brother. There was no mention of a son, legitimate or otherwise.

But the star witness for the prosecution was the London barrister Charles Challen, called as an expert on English law. Challen had thick black hair and a sharp, slightly foxy face, and he wooed Sioux City by appearing in black robes and a powdered wig adorned with pink silk tassels, the full regalia of the Inner Temple. He'd lost an arm fighting in France during the war, and his charming manner had both flair and dash. He created sympathy on the stand, where his delivery was droll and superior.

"No, no, no sir, no, *no!*" he exclaimed when Harry Reed asked him if there existed in England such a body as the "King's and Lords' Commission." Challen's accent—honed by years of work in the English courts, by study at Trinity, the richest and most prestigious of the Cambridge University colleges, by service in a top regiment of the Royal Artillery—could cut glass. It cut Hartzell. "No, by God, no sir, NO!"

Charles Challen sounded like the Scarlet Pimpernel.

Harry Reed wrote:

Challen was firmly convinced that water was fatal except for bathing and that under no circumstances could American water be taken internally. He further announced that a quart of intoxicating liquor was essential to him daily and, in its absence, he would not be able to testify. It was in the middle of the prohibition era. He did testify. After his return to England he was a member of Parliament for a time but never lost his aversion to water as a beverage.

We get the picture. The State Department was paying for Challen's trip, and giving him a hefty fee, and had auditioned a number of candidates for this particular job before settling on him. He was like a virtuoso English character, and he was expected to give a dazzling performance. He did. Carlos Goltz, who came to regard Challen as a soul mate from across the ocean, later said ruefully that the two of them together would have made an unstoppable team.

Challen's testimony was technical and precise, and all the lawyers, including Goltz and the rest of the defense team and even Judge Scott, were impressed. This was the legal nitty-gritty, mouthpieced by a class act. Challen denounced as utter fiction Hartzell's most exuberant statements, not just those concerning the "Lord and King's Commission" but the notion that "the Ecclesiastical Courts" could be involved in a probate case.

"There would be a revolution if the people of Britain thought they had jurisdiction over such a matter," he said. He punctured "the powers that be" with a sigh, saying quietly: "I find that a very odd notion indeed."

He said that even if everything Hartzell said was true (and of course he thought it was fraudulent balderdash), even if Hartzell had discovered a rival heir to the Drake Estate, even if it could be proved that Queen Elizabeth had taken more than her fair share of Drake's gold, even if all this was true, then no claim could be made because the statute of limitations had expired some hundreds of years ago, twelve years after the date of Drake's death to be precise.

Anyway, Challen said, referring to the claim that Elizabeth had robbed Drake of his gold, Drake had stolen the gold from the Spaniards in the first place and there was a law in England prohibiting a thief, or the heirs of a thief, from trying to recover his stolen property. A highwayman who had tried that back in the seventeenth century soon found himself at the end of a rope.

Moreover, he went on, even if Colonel Drexel Drake were the true heir, and even if the British government were about to hand over those billions and billions of pounds (an idea that was nonsense, he said), even if all this were also true (and it wasn't), then it was not legally possible for Colonel Drake to make an assignment of the whole package to Oscar Merrill Hartzell or anyone else.

This looked bad for Hartzell.

Now came the secret witness Mr. X, none other than the private eye Thomas Barnard. On hearing of Hartzell's arrest and deportation, Barnard had volunteered his story and his services as a witness to the American embassy. He too was in Sioux City on State Department expenses, and Harry Reed led him through the story of what had happened at the American Bar at the Savoy and during the ensuing drinking session at Basil Street, when Hartzell had apparently said the whole scheme was "a racket."

When it was his turn, Goltz sprang to his feet so threateningly the *Sioux City Tribune* described him next day as "fire-eating Carlos Goltz." Here was a witness to chew up and spit out smoking.

"You're a private detective," Goltz said. "That means you lie for a living?"

Goltz rightly regarded Thomas Barnard's testimony as highly suspect. It didn't come out in court what Barnard's relationship to Mrs. St. John Montague was, or in what way she benefited from having him follow Hartzell, but Goltz was easily able to suggest that whatever the two of them were up to it was no good. Unfortunately Goltz then committed one of the classic mistakes of cross-examination—asking a question to which he did not know the answer.

Barnard stated that in London Hartzell lived the life of an English gentleman.

Goltz said: "How does an English gentleman live?"

Barnard answered: "Hartzell had two women pregnant at the same time."

Goltz had this smart (and probably untrue) response struck from the record, but once again damage had been done.

———

Goltz told Hartzell to plead insane, but Hartzell, indignant, threw his arms in the air and declined. He didn't understand the suggestion at all. So Goltz based the defense on the creation of a presumption of Hartzell's good intent and by plunging into greater and ever foggier details with regard to historical facts and legal technicalities, creating chaos out of order in the jurors' minds. It was a good plan.

He called a procession of witnesses from Minnesota, from the Dakotas, from Texas, from Illinois, from Iowa itself, more than twenty witnesses in all, each of them testifying as to his or her unwavering faith in the man they'd taken to calling "the Big Chief"; and he landed blows during a three-hour reexamination of Charles Challen, the heaviest coming when he forced Challen to concede that the English statute of limitations had not until recently applied to a legal procedure for the reclamation of property known as "a petition of right," the name for a certain type of suit against the British Crown. This was the very procedure Hartzell had often claimed to be employing to press his claim for the Drake Estate. Yes, Challen admitted, the law bringing petitions of right within the conventional statute of limitations had been passed by Parliament only in 1925.

Goltz to Challen: "Did you ever read what purported to be a letter from Hartzell to someone in this country calling attention to that parliamentary Act and saying, 'No wonder they passed that law.' "

Challen: "I heard it read, that surprised me very much."

The implication here was that this new law had been passed precisely to prevent Hartzell lodging such a claim. Clearly Oscar had made himself as knowledgeable about English law as he was about American. The business about the petition of right was shrewd, and Goltz tried to ram home the good impression by calling his own expert on English law, P. J. Cahill, an Irish attorney now practicing in Chicago.

Goltz asked Cahill: "What is the basis for a petition of right?"

Harry Reed rose to object: the question was immaterial, he said, since no evidence had been produced that Hartzell had lodged a petition of right or even tried to lodge one.

This was a catastrophe for the defense. Up until now the jury had been able to envision the possibility of Hartzell's making and winning a case about the Drake Estate in England, and would have had reason therefore to accept his good faith. This reason now vanished: during all the time he'd been in England, Hartzell had taken no legal action to pursue the estate; unlike Milo Lewis, he'd never even gone through the motions.

The defense collapsed, and in closing, Goltz ceased to refer to history or legal niceties and relied on blunt emotional manipulation.

"The government has tried to alarm you," he said. "They have told you that if such a thing as establishing this claim were possible, no property in the world would be safe. If it had been a few years ago that kind of argument would have worried me. But they don't seem to realize they've already taken your farms away from you.

"Hartzell never took a farm from anyone except his own mother. Let me tell you, this man who has called the government officials crooks when they stole his papers, this man who has given the best years of his life to this one thing, who has fought with such zealousness, who has had but one thought—the Drake Estate, either he is telling you the truth or he is crazy—an absolute lunatic.

"Everyone has a right to his own ideas. No matter how visionary or foolish they may seem. If I plan an expedition to the moon and others become interested with me, they have a right to join me in the enterprise and I have the right to receive aid from them, providing I believe in my scheme.

"Let me tell you. The people in Iowa have as much right to invest their money in a project to establish a claim to an ancient estate, regardless of how impossible it seems, as they have in New York to go down and invest their money in Wall Street.

"These donators are like the people who assisted Columbus in his expedition or any other of the numerous occasions in history when persons have stood together and accomplished that which everyone was saying was impossible and couldn't be done.

"But the government says we must not try such things. We must stay at home on our farms and hoe and hoe and hoe so that Wall Street can get all our money."

The people of Iowa are good and right and the government is pernicious and wrong, and never forget that Oscar Hartzell is one of you and on your side, Goltz told the jurors, and he had good reason to believe the tactic would be successful. The packed courtroom was silent, breathless, as Harry Reed rose to his feet to answer for the government.

"Hartzell rose to new heights in Mr. Goltz's argument," he said. "He was like Columbus—only Columbus did discover America. He was like Lindbergh flying the Atlantic—only Lindbergh flew the Atlantic. And we've waited ten years for Hartzell to get somewhere and he still is making promises he does not and cannot keep."

He read portions from forty-eight of the letters and telegrams that Hartzell had written. In Reed's flat, dry voice, Hartzell's claims and excuses sounded doubly absurd.

"Silence! Mystery! Nondisturbance! This man is a master in the psychology of fraud. One might as well believe in *The Arabian Nights* as to believe in this man.

"Promises! Promises! Promises! Fraud from start to finish and he knew it. If this man goes out of here with the endorsement of this jury the state of Iowa will pay millions more tribute to him."

The case went to the jury at two o'clock in the afternoon of November 14, and nine and a half hours later a verdict still had not been reached. That night, Hartzell as usual enjoyed dinner in the most prominent spot in the dining room of the Martin Hotel, like a prince enjoying his last fling with the dungeon waiting for him at dawn.

Early the next morning the jury reached its decision and came back in. Standing before the bench, Hartzell, so imperturbable, even insouciant, throughout the trial, appeared calm but pale.

He was found guilty by a unanimous verdict on all counts.

Goltz asked to make a statement before sentencing. "I merely wish to inform the court, Your Honor, that the defendant is fifty-seven years old and is suffering from kidney trouble."

With that Goltz sat down, and so did Hartzell, only to be told to get back on his feet. For a minute, confused, he looked about him, then put a hand on the counsel table for support and heaved himself to his feet. It was then, he later said, that he looked around the court and saw the ominous figure of Judge Graves, an old adversary from London, Sudie Whittaker's legal ally, "one *hell* of a piece of timber"; he began to wonder whether Whittaker and Lewis had, after all, somehow brought about his demise.

In a slow, quiet voice, Judge Scott commended the jury for resisting the various pressures they'd no doubt felt and for bringing in a verdict which, he believed, was the only one possible. He sentenced Hartzell to ten years in Leavenworth, plus a $2,000 fine.

Hartzell, again enraged by the world's shocking failure to fall in line with his will, replaced his previously smiling attitude to the press with a snarl. "I have no statement to make," he said, and refused to pose for pictures. "I'm in jail. I'm through."

Next day the *Sioux City Journal* revenged itself by printing a doctored version of the classy studio portrait Hartzell had handed out. The *Journal*'s artroom superimposed heavy bars on the picture, so that Hartzell peered between them like a monkey in a cage. The *Journal* caption ran: "A beaten man, Oscar M. Hartzell, deposed and disconsolate 'baron' of the Drake Estate myth, gazed through jail bars Wednesday out upon a world that in his eyes is cruel and unrelenting."

But if Hartzell thought he was through, Carlos Goltz was not. He asked Judge George Scott to let Hartzell out on bail, pending appeal. Scott declined, so Goltz flew at once to Omaha, Nebraska, where he roused another federal judge to challenge Scott's bail decision. This time he won. Federal circuit judge J. W. Woodrough set Hartzell's bail at $25,000, despite impassioned pleas from the government.

Within hours bail was met, Hartzell was free, and, incredibly, the swindle started up all over again, with yet greater gusto.

Drake headquarters were removed from Des Moines to a secret address in Chicago, and a fund was launched for Hartzell's appeal. Within days scores of thousands of dollars had been donated.

A Des Moines office worker, Miss B. Dahlberg, explained that she refused to give up on Hartzell because she knew he'd been framed by powerful unseen interests. "The whole Drake deal would have been fixed up by now if it weren't for that bunch of racketeers they sent over from Washington. Those men at the trial are just sore because they can't get in on it," she said.

Dahlberg was an unbending Drake fundamentalist. She spoke about "O.M." in a hushed voice, as though he were distant and almost godlike, a financial genius, a giant of a leader whose existence and acumen so threatened the power of the authorities in both America and England that they were terrified of him. She said she thought his appeal would take about a year, and by then, she predicted, he would have gone to England again and come back with the fortune, enriching the chosen and stopping the mouths of his vile critics. "It'll happen soon. I have all the confidence in the world," she said.

Meetings continued to be held, in farmhouses, or outside in the fields, at night, lit by torches and car headlamps. Sometimes Hartzell came from Chicago for these meetings, in which case there was tense excitement. He didn't speak much. He told the faithful he was a thinker, not a speaker, but had thought hard and long. He told them that England was gathering money to liquidate the debt, that this was indeed why the British had come off the gold standard, and that, as they all knew, the Depression would not be settled until the Drake Estate was settled. He concerned himself only with the loftiest and most solemn pronouncements, while the previously reviled Otto Yant stood by his side and proved a firebrand orator. Hartzell looked on benignly as Yant told the crowds that Postmaster General Farley's recent trip to Europe had been in the interests of settling the estate. Farley had told his subordinates to lay off the case, because the government had nothing on Hartzell. Yant held up a receipt saying that the notorious Post Office inspector John Sparks had himself donated $5—another deft touch. Moreover, after months of holding up the settlement, President Roosevelt had at last stopped wavering and come down on their side. Roosevelt's supposed fishing vacation in the Bahamas was really "a secret meeting with British financial figures in order to finish the deal." Huey Long's "every-man-a-king" and "share-the-wealth" radio speeches confirmed that things looked good for the Drakers. The social and financial and political implications were mind-boggling they reached so far. If Vice-President Dawes was shown in a newspaper lighting a pipe, it was a sign that distribution was imminent.

Walt Whitman said that faith was the antiseptic of the soul. "It pervades the common people and preserves them. They never give up expecting and believing and trusting," he wrote. Smacked by the Depression, enraged at government, spurred and lifted only by the vision of the doubloons and gems and gold in Drake's fortune, Hartzell's people became a band of barmy crusaders. At rallies across the Midwest there were talks on God and the world as it ought to be.

"It's all connected with the New Deal," wrote one acolyte. "If you can figure out just where and when President Roosevelt is going to get money to finance the NRA you will know when we can expect our checks. The two deals are very closely connected. This may not make good sense to you, but nevertheless it is the whole story."

In Alton, Iowa, speaking of the Drake Estate, the Lutheran minister Palmer S. Nestander said that all the people in his neighborhood "ate it, drank it, slept it." Nor was the Rev. Palmer Nestander opposed: he had given money himself, had got his church board in, and was sending bales of cash to Chicago. The Sioux City trial hadn't deterred him in the least. "Of course they hate Hartzell," he said. "He's our hero."

Hartzell had tried to think of himself only as a businessman, as a figure along the lines of Andrew Mellon or J. P. Morgan—but now he'd become Robin Hood, stealing from the rich to give to the poor. Except, of course, he kept the money for himself.

Harry Reed saw that his part of the world had gone through the looking glass. He wrote:

After Hartzell was convicted and while he was out on bail, a lawyer from Des Moines and Hartzell's brother Canfield conducted a campaign for funds to continue the appeal. The attorney told me that they got $150,000. He said that arrangements had been made for the attorney and Hartzell to go to England, get the estate and all the money from the British and bring it back in complete vindication of Hartzell. Hartzell, his brother, and the attorney went to New York with the brother carrying the bag with the $150,000 in it. They stood on the dock, the boat whistled, Hartzell put his arm around the attorney and held him and Hartzell's brother left for Europe with the money. I asked the attorney if he did not think it was all a bit fantastic and he said that after the brother left with the money he began to think that maybe it was.

The Sioux City conviction was upheld by a circuit court of appeals on August 16, 1934, and Hartzell, undaunted, at once determined to appeal to the U.S. Supreme Court. By then he was drinking hard and living in Chicago at the Croydon Hotel, where he was visited regularly by P. J. Cahill, the Irish attorney who'd been Carlos Goltz's expert on English law. Other times Hartzell would drop by Cahill's office, not for legal advice, but to talk. Cahill, who came from Tipperary and had attended Jesuit school, at first found Hartzell a fascinating study, but then they became friends.

Cahill said: "Knowing that I was Irish, he told me that he would buy Ireland from England and give the Irish their independence; he told me that, if I married the lady who accompanied me on an occasion when we had dinner together, he would buy her a castle; he told me, when we were pouring out a drink, that 'this was the way that Cave, Lord Cave, used to do it in England'; he also told me that this was not the proper way to pour wine, that wine should come out of a tea kettle; he told me that the Pope was tying up the Drake Estate and that the Pope was trying to steal his gold and had gold belonging to him in the Vatican; he told me that the Pope and the King of England had joined hands and were stopping the final determination of the settlement; he told me that President Roosevelt had been compelled to gather in all the gold in America for the purpose of paying him."

On learning that the child of one of Cahill's friends was upset because a dog or cat had killed her black rabbits, Hartzell told him to promise the little girl that when the Drake Estate was settled he would buy her all the black rabbits in the world. He told him he was also going to make sure that a large part of the state of Iowa would be set aside for his family and friends so that as long as they lived they would enjoy milk and honey. He told him he no longer believed in the dollar; he was sending all his monies to New York and having them converted into English and Canadian currency, and he advised the Irishman to do likewise.

On December 3, 1934, the Supreme Court refused to intervene, and Hartzell was given a deadline to return to Sioux City and surrender himself so he could begin his term at Leavenworth.

"The highest powers that be will step in," he told Cahill confidently. But the weeks slipped by, the highest powers didn't, and the appointed hour came around. It was January 12, 1935, and Hartzell was still determined to be debonair. At six in the evening he called

Cahill and suggested they go out for a final, splendid dinner, but by the time Cahill arrived at the Croydon, Hartzell was raving drunk.

"I did not accept the invitation. His condition was such that I did not want to be with him. He was then utterly and hopelessly incapable of realizing the seriousness of his position or anything else serious at all," Cahill said.

Hartzell was alone when, at the stroke of midnight, the police rapped on the door. He refused to let them in and called Cahill in a panic. Cahill said there was nothing else for it—he had to give himself up.

He was taken to the Chicago Avenue station, so distressed that guards took his belt and suspenders away from him and kept a watch throughout the night lest he try suicide.

On Monday morning a federal marshal arrived to transport him to Leavenworth. Hartzell was in much better form; as usual he'd faced the crisis and recovered some aplomb. He demanded that they take a taxi. The federal marshal replied that they would be riding in a truck. Hartzell said he was worried he might catch cold.

"You'll have plenty of time to get over it," the marshal said.

"You don't understand. I'll be out within days. Roosevelt himself's going to see to it," Hartzell said.

SIX

Flight into Madness

O n starting my research I was told that Hartzell's Bureau of Prisons file had been destroyed during a routine culling of government documents during the 1970s. This blow only heightened the glee I felt much later when I discovered that the file hadn't been burned after all, but had been pulled, saved, and reclassified at the National Archives under the promising category "Notorious Offenders." This file, nine folders of documents in all, contained Hartzell's autobiography and numerous psychiatric evaluations, as well as the routine prison stuff. It was like opening a pirate's chest.

The file revealed that Hartzell arrived at Leavenworth on January 16, 1935, and was given the inmate number 46137-L. His profession was listed as "financier." He looked ten years younger than his age, then fifty-nine.

The file revealed that Hartzell adjusted to prison life quickly. He was described as "Neat in personal appearance, affable, quick, and eager in response. He is apparently frank, but with some reservations pertaining to secrets of vital importance which, if known, would destroy trusts and render impotent his well-formulated plans."

The file revealed that a psychiatrist noted dryly: "This man has received an immense amount of publicity which he seems to enjoy."

The file revealed, amazingly, that even Hartzell's removal to Leavenworth put scarcely a dent in the scheme, because many people refused to believe that he was in Leavenworth at all.

A reporter from the *Des Moines Tribune* wrote to Leavenworth warden Fred Herbst to ask if he might visit the prison and see Hartzell with his own eyes so he could assure his readers of the real situation: "As you may know, this man has swindled Iowa simple-folk out of more than $1m. These same people are now sending their hard earned money to Hartzell's lieutenants in the belief that Hartzell walked in one door of Leavenworth and out another. The story is that the government is afraid of Hartzell and dare not imprison him."

A Milwaukee attorney wrote: "While it is generally known that Oscar M. Hartzell is confined in your institution as a result of his conviction for using the United States Mails to defraud, nevertheless, it appears that his agents and confederates in the notorious Sir Francis Drake Estate swindle have been, are now, and in all probability will continue to be successful in making a considerable number of innocent and extremely gullible people in Wisconsin believe that Hartzell has never been and is not now confined in your institution, but that he is presently in England to conclude the negotiations for the transfer of the assets of the estate of Sir Francis Drake to this country for distribution."

From Topeka, Kansas, Senator Arthur Capper added another twist: "The suggestion is made that Hartzell is being granted special privileges at the penitentiary, such as being given quarters at the home of the warden, meals sent in, a private telephone, etc."

This beggared belief, and Warden Herbst wrote to Senator Capper: "I beg leave to advise you that Hartzell is employed here as a cleaner in 'B' cell house, scrubbing floors, etc. He is about sixty years old. He occupies a cell, five by nine feet, in that cell house. He has not been, and is not now, receiving any privileges not accorded any other prisoner confined here. He has not been outside of the penitentiary since his commitment."

Fred Herbst was clearly flummoxed and exasperated, but his attempts to straighten the record were of little avail. Even scrubbing the floor of his prison cell, Hartzell had that quality known as prestige, and at this point in time it paralyzed people's critical faculties. He'd said what he said so often that not only did they completely believe what he said; they were prepared to accept the most outlandish fictions about him. He was like Napoleon on Elba—everyone held his breath until he should return and conquer. Hartzell was such a figure in Iowa that he had his own impostor—a man was arrested who'd been traveling the state, collecting money, and claiming that he was Oscar Hartzell.

In Chicago, day-to-day command of the Drake operation was in the hands of Delmar Short, an Illinois man who'd lost his farm in 1931 and whose family had known hunger. Short was rebellious and controlling, an excellent mathematician with rhetorical skills. "It was a racket from top to bottom and I always knew it was a racket but I ran the racket because those were hard times," he said later. Short kept the books, controlled the secret office, and issued the following message:

"I will say our deal is going fine. This last stunt of taking him away is all in the play. We have been advised all along that the outside world would think this is a fraud. If the papers came out and said the Drake Estate was okay, we would be run to death by agents and grafters and some of our heavy donors would have trouble with kidnappers. As to Hartzell, he is not where the papers say, even though he left Chicago with officers. We know where he is and we know the reason."

Short wrote in a soothing, aw-shucks tone to another donor: "I think someone overstepped their authority in arresting him and have found it out and don't know what to do. We have advice from the Secret Service not to worry. So I guess everything will come out OK."

To another: "Now Mrs. Anderson do not worry about our deal. It is going to be settled and paid just as sure as the sun will rise in the morning."

And another: "Tell your wife, 'Chins up.' "

And: "We will have the money within sixty days, before the chickens are big enough to fry, although I do like fried chicken. It makes my mouth water just to write about it."

Delmar Short was very good: the years 1934–35 produced about $500,000 for the swindle and many wild instances of faith gone awry. Some believed Hartzell was being protected by agents of the Secret Service from hired gunmen in the pay of panic-stricken international financiers. A Post Office inspector in Galveston was told that a boat lying in the Gulf of Texas was filled with gold, a first payment from England. The inspector got several Drakers to go with him to the boat, where they saw it was loaded with oil pipes. The Drakers were unimpressed. They said they knew a government trick when they saw one—the gold must have been removed in the night.

In Adrian, Minnesota, it was reckoned that 75 to 90 percent of the population still believed that Hartzell was unstoppable and the Drake Estate would pay out eventually. Like many others, they refused to believe that he was in prison. The trial had been a smoke screen, a gigantic farce to cover up the fact that he was too big for the government to handle. A Minneapolis paper reported:

Drake estate enthusiasts, now talking about a semi-religious cult known as the "New Order" believe in the project fanatically. In some sections it is dangerous to point out the facts of the swindle. There have been street fights in Adrian and many bitter enmities have sprung up over "the Drake." Businessmen have been threatened with boycotting unless they give donations to the cause. Even those firmly convinced of the fraud consider it wise to refrain from discussion.

In Adrian, families were ruined and some of the richest people in town lost everything. For years afterward, whenever Adrian people voiced foolish dreams of getting rich, they would say, "When my Drake Estate comes in . . ."

In Washington a letter arrived on Roosevelt's desk. It was from Mrs. Troy Bookout, of Santa Rosa, Texas. Having been promised $40,000, she had invested $1 in the Drake Estate and was now at her wit's end, wondering when she would get the money, because her five children had nothing to eat. "No one but God and myself knows how hard it was for us to live, daily we are doing without food."

In Auburn, Iowa, an estimated seven to ten thousand people paid $1 each to attend a two-day meeting on a farm where plans were outlined for building clubs, golf links, swimming pools, playgrounds, and game preserves for the exclusive use of the Drakers after they had received their share of the estate. They dreamed of creating their own community—another America, for the hardworking but beleaguered folk of the Midwest.

In New York, meanwhile, armored trucks rolled up to the Riverside Drive apartment of Canfield Hartzell and deposited cash in large amounts: $10,000, $20,000, even, on one occasion, more than $50,000 in a single truckload. The Runyonesque Canfield never satisfactorily explained what became of all this loot, the Drake donations that were collected and sent to him during the years 1933–35, more than $300,000 delivered to him personally in all. Much of the money, he claimed, went to Oscar's bank account in Montreal. Some was sent to Hartzell's confederate W. J. Stewart in England, using the name C. Ray as shipper. This was very witty, Consul Guy Ray having been Hartzell's archfoe and nemesis at the

American embassy in London. Nobody, whether from the State Department or Scotland Yard or the Post Office, had any luck figuring out what the valet Stewart did with his end, although he did admit to Detective Arthur Bishop that he had "come into some money," the source of which he unsurprisingly refused to divulge, leaving Bishop to suppose he probably had not been left it in the will of a favorite aunt. Stewart, then, got lucky. It's also very likely Canfield pocketed large sums for himself.

Authorities didn't see how to put an end to it. They knew that the Sioux City trial had backfired, and that the swindlers had set up operations away from Iowa—they suspected Chicago, but they didn't know where, and Hartzell, of course, was not prepared to oblige with the information.

Then the Chicago police caught a break. Someone found a letter in the street and handed it in. The letter, from Frank Butterbrodt in Beaver Dam, Wisconsin, was addressed to Butterbrodt's nephew, a medical student at Northwestern University named Roland Schoen. Butterbrodt asked Schoen to go check on an investment he'd made—and he gave an address.

Posing as Schoen, Detective James Zagar went to an office on Rush Street, just three blocks from where Hartzell had lived at the Croydon Hotel. Zagar realized he'd stumbled on the headquarters of the Drake swindle, and five days later, on April 8, he led a raid, arresting everybody on the premises, eight people, including Short, Otto Yant, and Lester Ohmart, Hartzell's man in Texas. One of the eight, Joseph Hauber, inspired by Hartzell's old Mogford wheeze, boldly tried to pass himself off as a Scotland Yard detective, saying he'd been tracking this outfit for years and had been on the point of tipping off the authorities when he was caught in the raid. This might have worked in Iowa, but not in cynical Chicago; Zagar shrugged, grinned, and slapped the cuffs on Hauber anyway. Another, James Kirkendall, a man of sixty-six, died of a heart attack immediately after being arraigned.

The situation didn't lack drama. All records were seized, including the sucker list—seventy thousand names. In Yant's desk, Zagar found the day's cash receipts; more than $7,500 was stuffed in a drawer. An American Express messenger, who arrived when police were searching the premises, refused to leave a package containing more than $12,000. A further $31,000 was found in hotel rooms back at the Croydon. And James Kirkendall's safe deposit box in the vault of the Capitol building surrendered $13,000 in U.S. bills and a further $1,173 in English money.

There was also a letter that Delmar Short had been writing. It was still in the typewriter.

Mr. Koelker,

No doubt you have heard by this time that April 8th is the last day for finance on this deal. After that day books will be closed forever and then it will take about four and a half months to get to the donators. This isn't much news but I think it is pretty good news and there will not be any more until you get your settlement. Thanking you very kindly. I am yours very truly, DG Short.

Short had been hustling hard, running a final drive for donations before shutting up shop for good. The "four and a half months" was neat, leaving an ample window for escape.

James Zagar and his men had closed in at the death. A few more days and Short and the rest would have been gone.

In an effort to stamp out the swindle for good, the net of prosecution was thrown very wide indeed. During the next months more and more people were indicted—forty-one in all. And Oscar Hartzell was fetched from his five-by-nine-foot cell in Leavenworth to face trial yet again, this time in Chicago.

He saw familiar and unwelcome faces.

Charles Challen, the droll one-armed barrister, was brought over once again to testify on English law. As a sign of his prestige, Challen asked to be paid in gold guineas, ten a day, plus expenses. He traveled in a first-class stateroom with sitting room and bathroom attached on the *Île de France* and while in Chicago gave a series of lectures. This time the State Department decided to back up Challen with a Scotland Yard man, rather than the private detective Thomas Barnard, and Arthur Bishop, by then promoted from sergeant to the rank of inspector, was given the assignment.

Bishop was youthful, brisk, and, above all, dapper. He arrived in Chicago carefully dressed in a double-breasted gray suit with spats. Courted by the press, he promptly had a rush of blood to the head. A reporter asked what he thought of the FBI's handling of the John Dillinger case (Dillinger having been gunned down outside the Biograph Theater during the summer of the previous year), and Bishop replied that Scotland Yard preferred to bring in its men alive. "I'd have used charm and finesse," he said. "I'd have offered Dillinger a cigarette." It's not clear whether Bishop was joking, but there was uproar, and FBI director J. Edgar Hoover himself became involved, writing a letter which now resides in Hartzell's Scotland Yard file. He wanted the Yard to rest assured that the FBI didn't blaze away at just anybody. He pointed out that Dillinger had a record of violence, and was armed and reaching for a weapon at the time of his death.

And so on: Hoover's letter was a model of restraint and forbearance; probably he felt deference to the then unassailed reputation of Scotland Yard. Bishop was told to keep his mouth shut or lose his job, and was never promoted again, becoming another, albeit minor, victim of the lunacy which, like some heady gas, seemed to overcome anyone associated too long with Oscar Hartzell and the Sir Francis Drake Estate.

The trial, which opened on November 18, 1935, before Justice Philip L. Sullivan, repeated many elements of the first, although at greater length and expense and with a cast whose size would have warmed the heart of Cecil B. DeMille. Sullivan grew irritable when he saw that witnesses took to sitting with their friends at the defendants' table, further increasing the crowd and causing confusion. The Drakers wanted to show they were sticking together, but this was also a planned ploy, a demonstration that they refused to take the prosecution seriously, the gesture of people who had ceased to believe in the benevolence of the system.

The defense, conducted by Edward J. Hess and George M. Crane (who both at one point tried to withdraw, saying they hadn't been paid and their clients were unruly), ceased to insist on the reality of the estate and the Drake heir and instead tried to show good faith. In this Hess and Crane were largely successful. On January 13, 1936, when the trial had already been running several weeks, Judge Sullivan concluded that many of those accused believed absolutely in the Drake Estate and freed twenty-one of them with these words: "To defendants who are going to be found not guilty: if you have sinned, go ye and sin no more, and don't be sinned against any more. Go back to your hamlets, villages, your cities, and tell all those people, the donors and contributors, that the court has judicially found that there is no pot of gold at the end of the rainbow." On January

31, twelve more were acquitted. This time Sullivan said: "There never was a goose that laid a golden egg. Sir Francis Drake is dead. Let him rest in peace. Don't try to revive him."

The trial went on, only eight defendants remaining now, Hartzell preeminent among them. He listened while Challen, Bishop, Dr. Arthur Lyon Cross of the University of Michigan, and C. Percy Powell from the Library of Congress did their stuff, and he heard, again, the reading of the true will of Sir Francis Drake. The donors loyally stood their ground, clinging to their hopes in spite of everything. One said: "With all due respect to the court, I haven't changed my mind. There were seventy thousand in the deal and they have taken only one. From what I hear the deal is as solid as the Rock of Gibraltar."

But the climax of the second trial involved Hartzell's brothers. A surprise prosecution witness, Clinton Hartzell traveled from his farm in Minnesota to testify about the stormy meeting that had taken place in the Great Northern Hotel in Chicago more than a decade before.

He said, "Oscar said he was breaking with the Whittaker-Lewis organization. They had operated the racket for many years. He wanted me to go in with him. I told him I wanted nothing to do with the rotten Drake Estate. Oscar said, 'Why not quit working so hard and make some easy money? We can clean up a million easy.'"

Clinton was a tall, lanky, gray-haired man who spoke slowly and believably. He also testified as to the conversation he'd had with Canfield at their mother's funeral in Monmouth in 1924. "I told him he would be in the penitentiary and he said, 'Hell, that's the trouble with you—you're always scared. What's the difference? The government can't touch us.'" And then, as if to damn the entire rest of his family, he quoted his sister, Pearl Palmer, as saying: "I know it's a fraud but Mother sent money and Oscar is collecting and I'll take it.

I know it's a swindle but I married a poor man and I'm going to get some dough."

Clinton Hartzell was a diligent and honest man, but all the same this was a remarkable betrayal. He'd long been angered by Oscar's arrogance; perhaps he resented the money sent Canfield's and Pearl's way while none had come his, and had determined to weed out the dishonesty in his family or have revenge upon them all. There was talk too of a feud over a loan Clinton had made to their mother. Families and finance often make melancholy companions, and thereafter Oscar refused to acknowledge the bond, referring to Clinton as a "found" or "adopted" child, even though some records indicate he was a blood brother.

Hartzell still refused to take the stand in his own defense, and the trial, which had lasted eleven weeks, moved toward an end. This time too there was uncertainty as to the outcome, but Hartzell, Delmar Short, Lester Ohmart, Joseph Hauber (despite his Mogford alibi), Canfield Hartzell, A. R. Gregory, and Emil Rochel were found guilty by a jury that deliberated seven hours and dramatically filed back in at eleven at night to give its verdict in the otherwise deserted federal building.

Canfield was the first to be sentenced, and when Oscar heard Judge Sullivan give his brother five years, something inside him snapped. At last he told his attorney Ed Hess he wanted to address the court.

Hess said to Sullivan: "This man is possessed of an obsession and if he talks he will probably save the other defendants."

Hartzell rose to his feet and said: "I'm responsible for all this. All they did was take the money. The people who worked for me are all innocent."

Sullivan, silver-haired and shortsighted and of impish urbanity, decided to draw Hartzell out. Or was he teasing? He asked if King

George V had been involved with the deal. The king had died only a few days before.

Hartzell studied the judge for a second. "Judge, your honor, we never quote the king—it just isn't done. I wouldn't tell that to anybody, it just isn't done—but you can read between the lines, can't you?" he said in a hushed tone.

One of the prosecutors interrupted to say that Hartzell had spent much of the $1,500,000 he'd been sent on women and riotous living in London.

"That's a lie. It's a lie," Hartzell shouted.

This was superb stuff. Judge Sullivan asked, "How big is the Drake Estate?"

"It's beyond anyone's imagination," said Hartzell in a wild voice. "If I disclosed anything about it now I'd be a traitor. All the money would be lost. I'm sworn to secrecy by the highest powers. They run the country over there."

Sullivan reduced Canfield's jail term to a year and a day, gave Short, Ohmart, Hauber, Gregory, and Rochel the same sentence, and ordered Hartzell to undergo immediate mental evaluation.

Before he was taken away to the cells, Delmar Short was asked what he thought would become of Hartzell. "Jesus Christ was just one man," said Short with his customary rhetorical flair. "But they crucified him too."

Hartzell now fell into the hands of psychiatrists. They had to find out if he was mad, and if so when he'd gone mad and how mad he really was, or if he was faking it. Even today, on a consideration of all the available evidence, this is no easy task.

The first to take a crack was Dr. Harry Hoffman, director of the Cook County Criminal Court Behavior Clinic. A *Chicago Tribune* photograph of Hoffman showed a lean sharp-featured man with a neat little mustache and brilliantined black hair that came to a point on a wide forehead. In this picture his eyes were puffy and black-rimmed from lack of sleep. He looked scary and vampiric, like Bela Lugosi rising from his coffin, but then being called upon in 1936 to evaluate just which of Chicago's criminals might or might not be insane doubtless required steely, if not supernatural, qualities of character and resolve. With Hartzell he did a cool and businesslike job.

"I'll have to go back to England," Hartzell told Hoffman. "If you come over there with me—I'll do my best—if you hooked up with me, money is no object. I'm pretty good-hearted to my friends. I'd turn you loose over there. I think you'd like to know me over there. You just come, and leave the rest to me. You don't have to take any of your money, I'll take care of that. If a man can't make any money with his finger on a trigger like that, well . . ."

Hartzell said maybe it was a good thing he was in the penitentiary for the moment, for otherwise the financial interests would pop him off.

"It's a huge amount. It's double 130 billions. That's sterling. I don't think it will be liquidated in cash. I'll have to settle with England and England will have to settle with me and then I become Francis Drake. I'll get the name of Francis Drake. There are no great adventurers like him anymore. I'm Sir Francis Drake now."

Hoffman asked: "You never hear strange voices talking to you?"

"No, no—not at all."

"You're not here by any spiritual means at all?"

"Not that I know it—I'm just an ordinary man."

"You know why I'm here?"

"Yes, sure, to examine me."

"My name is what?"

"Hoffman," Hartzell said. "You know what's going on in Europe right now? What's the cause of it? What's the trouble in Ethiopia?"

"The Drake Estate?"

"Why of course."

He showed Hoffman a cartoon from the previous day's paper; it showed a farmer, hat pushed back from his forehead, approaching the Houses of Parliament in London. "The British White House. This is about me," he said. "Somebody had it in for me and tore this, the people upstairs. Jealousy always exists."

"Do you think you have some special mission to perform in this world?"

"That has never crossed my mind. I went in as a cold-blooded business proposition. I'll trade with you twenty-four hours a day if you'll let me make some money and you can make money. I'm a money man."

He said he'd been hounded by the Post Office but he had the power to stop the war in Ethiopia and ruin the British aristocracy and governments would topple and the structure of every nation's finances would shift and shake when he became the world's dominant economic figure. "This thing has already hurt J. P. Morgan bad. I am the mystery man—and they thought they were dealing with a hick farmer. Why it's just like an underground river, just cutting the ground all around and then you'll cave in. This deal is extraordinary, it's beyond the thoughts of man, but there she is. How long do you think they can keep me in jail after this thing pops? I'll get out just like a shot. I'm not worried a bit. My whole salvation is the finish of this deal."

If this was acting, it was a performance of cool nerve and outrageous effrontery, a galvanic projection. Hoffman concluded that

Hartzell was well oriented for time, place, and person. There was no evidence of hallucinations, but definite delusions of grandeur and persecution. Hoffman's diagnosis was: "Paranoid state. This patient is classifiable as insane."

Hartzell went back to Leavenworth, where the prison psychiatrist, Dr. D. E. Singleton, examined him again, noting that Hartzell was far more alert and sharp and intelligent in conversation than he appeared, or allowed himself to appear, from written tests. He was watchful and aware of his own performance, sculpting it to please.

Singleton wrote:

When specifically told that the uninformed naturally believe that this scheme was either a huge swindle or a delusion on his part, he states that he is aware of the fact, but that neither is the case, and that in the near future it would be shown that the Drake Estate is not a myth, but a reality. Whether this is a delusional system as a purposeful defensive mechanism, or a willful misstatement of facts, can hardly be determined at this time. No other suspicions of a psychosis are in evidence.

Singleton was less certain of madness than Hoffman had been, and he raised the possibility that Hartzell was putting it on, although he didn't have a strong enough suspicion of this to question Hoffman's judgment. The copy of his report in the Notorious Offenders file shows that his diagnosis—"Paranoia, grandiose and persecutory delusions"—was typed in some time after he completed the rest of the document, suggesting that he'd been reluctant to commit himself. In the end, however, Singleton was happy to rid himself of this troublesome freight, and he sat in on the meeting when it was decided to declare Hartzell insane and pass him along.

⌣

The final showdown came with Dr. Clark Mangun, head of psychiatry at the Hospital for Defective Delinquents in Springfield, Missouri. This was a new facility, built in the late 1920s, set in bucolic country in the Ozarks. The equipment was the best and most modern then available—the hospital had, for instance, one of the only two machines for measuring brain waves in America—but there was still a tension about whether the inmates should be seen as prisoners or sick people.

Clark Mangun, then in his fifties, was of the old school. Another Midwesterner, from Missouri, he had spent his entire career in the public health service. He was neither tough nor angry, a pleasant man by all accounts, but not prepared to put up with any nonsense. "There was no reason not to admire Dr. Clark Mangun," said Dr. Mortimer Ostaw, a psychologist and psychoanalyst who later worked with him. "He was a very formal man, a careful dresser. His wife always referred to him as 'Doctor.'" Yes, Mangun thought, Springfield was a hospital, but it was a hospital for delinquents.

Hartzell arrived there from Leavenworth on April 18, 1936, and was given the number 694 DD.

Because of the importance of the case and its peculiar circumstances, Mangun had orders to conduct an exhaustive study before Judge Sullivan passed sentence. So he sat with Hartzell for weeks on end, conducting a series of interviews; he wrote to everyone he could find who had known Hartzell in the past and might be prepared to give an opinion of him now. And he encouraged Hartzell to write an autobiography, a venture that Hartzell, imagining he was being invited to leave a statement for posterity rather than provide material for psychiatric evaluation, undertook with serious delight.

He thought his book would be published, an idea that pleased him. He assured Mangun it would be worth millions.

The reports, letters, assessments, and other papers that Mangun assembled told the story of a confrontation between two very different characters: the one, the doctor, was sober, orderly, neat, and unruffled as he sifted through the truth, lies, deceit, bluster, and probably madness that faced him; the other, the con man, was all psychological plumes and hectic color, eager to please, but with a flashing temper. The battle was intense and illuminating.

Mangun asked: "Of the two, would you prefer to be considered a swindling criminal or insane?"

Hartzell had no doubts. "I'd rather be considered a swindler."

"Why?"

"Because when my deal proved itself out, it would vindicate me. For people to say that a man is insane to attain their own ends—nothing lower in humanity could be done to any man when a man is helpless. And I would stop at nothing after I had redeemed myself to put everyone in the dungeons forever that had the slightest thing to do with it in any way," he said.

"Can't you see it might be to your advantage to be declared insane?"

"No sir! No sir!"

"If you're held of sound mind, they might sentence you to ten more years."

"Give me forty. Give me a hundred—give me a hundred years! It doesn't matter. I wish I'd told the judge in Chicago what I really had in mind but I was afraid to on account of protecting the others. I should have told him: 'Give me what you like, but you sentence one of the others and you'll spend the rest of your life behind bars. I'm talking about United States judges now—yourself. I'll be free.'

This thing is loaded with TNT and it's going to hit every fellow that's monkeyed with it. I've got nothing else to say. I guess I've said enough."

Hartzell's tetchy outburst ended that day's interview, but stories Mangun gathered from inmates confirmed and expanded the picture of delusion. With these other inmates he was prepared to talk off the cuff. He told them he had people hidden inside Springfield working for him. His food was being tested in case it was poisoned. The Bank of England, now owned by him, would be renamed the Empire Bank; similarly, the Canadian National Bank, another part of his far-reaching financial domain, would be called the Dominion Bank.

One inmate asked if he was like Croesus, the ancient king of Lydia, renowned for his great wealth.

Hartzell said he wasn't sure who Croesus was.

"Napoleon?"

Hartzell said Napoleon's power had been temporary while his own would be world-embracing and permanent.

He told another inmate slyly that he had $86,000 hidden away in Galva, Illinois, and $700,000 in Canada. This was more credible.

Of course, the idea of asking those who had already been termed criminally insane to report on another for the purpose of adjudging whether he was of the same condition was not without cruel irony, although the inmates to whom Mangun turned, "trusties," were carefully selected for their dependability and willingness to shape themselves to Springfield's routine of order and possible rehabilitation. Hartzell was not so prepared. He wasn't interested in any of that at all and refused to be bothered by his situation. He was euphoric, elated, exuberant. He came to the interviews, irritating the punctilious Mangun by appearing unshaven and with his shirt buttons undone and by pronouncing that he'd never felt better or been happier in his life. He refused to admit that he was wrong or a crook; nor did he express any regrets.

Mangun asked: "Do you wish you'd never heard of the Drake Estate? It's caused you so much trouble."

Hartzell was astonished by the question. "But all that trouble is what brought me my success. Bulldog nerve and not knowing how to be defeated. I went straight ahead, like a man in the deep river. You can't unhitch your horses in the middle of the stream," he said.

Mangun wrote grumpily:

In terms of prison jargon, this man has been a "loser." He is now starting to serve a ten year sentence, and he might with considerable good grace admit that he was a swindler of no mean proportions and boast of that accomplishment. But he stoutly maintains that his representations are *bona fide*, and shows every evidence of anticipating a settlement of the vast Drake Estate at any moment, at which time he will be fully vindicated, elevated to a higher position than any living mortal, and his enemies punished.

Here Mangun's no-nonsense values exposed a flaw in his logic: if Hartzell was mad, he wasn't capable of making the suggested choice; and if he wasn't, he was putting one over on the good doctor in a way that scarcely calls the word "loser" to mind. To act with "considerable good grace" was of less than considerable interest to Hartzell, and there were still those on the outside who thought that if he was crazy, he was crazy with a purpose.

C. F. Keeling, sheriff of Polk County, Iowa (the office for which Hartzell had run back in 1914), wrote to Mangun: "We suggest you take care that Hartzell does not resell your library or the Lake of the

Ozarks before he is released. His general reputation here, among the old timers, is BAD."

Mangun gave Hartzell IQ tests, U.S. Army intelligence tests, tests of word association, tests where he had to fit wooden blocks of various shapes into receptacles of corresponding sizes and shapes. When asked to define a balloon, Hartzell said, "Define means to make smaller, so stick a pin in it."

At the end of each day's interview, Hartzell read pages from his autobiography. Sometimes he couldn't wait to get going. Mangun observed: "He then read me about seven pages of manuscript that he had written of his dealings with the Drake Estate up to the point of his acquisition of control. This he read in a very forceful and pompous fashion."

It's the autobiography which is the best revelation of Hartzell's state of mind.

The con man's will to deceive is matched and enabled by his suckers' urge to believe. Their relationship is codependent, and it's also symbiotic. Information and emotion travel both ways, from the con man to the sucker, from sucker to con man, living off each other, and the con man must have a strong will and a clear head if he's to remain untouched by the cupidity of his victims. Insincerity is hard to keep up for a day, let alone for years, for decades. Yellow Kid Weil, for instance, had the knack, but then he was constantly switching stories as he moved from one likely scheme to the next. Hartzell was only ever involved with the one fiction. He was attracted to an idea—the Drake Estate—whose apostle and exploiter he then became. The pages of his autobiography, written in hand and then typed by Dr. Clark Mangun's secretary, show that in the end he became this idea's victim too. His attitude toward the scheme described a circle that started with belief, moved to cynical disbelief, and finally came back all the way. The Drake Estate hypnotized and possessed him.

When he was writing about his childhood, about his parents, about his life as a farmer, about his adventures in Madison County and Texas, Hartzell was clear and easy to understand, and his memories check out against the other existing sources. Even on the painful subjects of his years as a bankrupt and his early humiliations at the hands of Lewis and Whittaker, he remained grounded in reality.

But once he moved on to the subject of his running of the Drake scheme, the writing became excitable and obsessed, moving around and around in spirals of illusion, never allowing itself to dwell on any concrete detail. Because he obliterated the possibility of letting himself address what had really gone on during those years, because he was never going to write about bilking scores of thousands of his compatriots, about living the high life and how that made him feel, it was as if his mind split and would not allow itself to linger over anything else from that period. The intensity with which he propounded the faith made everything else vanish.

At one time he'd had to force himself to do this; but by the time he wrote his autobiography the process had become a part of him. The trumpets of Drake's fortune drowned out everything else. Factual details strayed in as if by accident, like table 101 at the Savoy, or the final farewell lunch with the Scotland Yard men at Simpson's, or the snow that fell on the Sunday morning he arrived in Sioux City, but most of the boiling, chaotic prose concerned the ins and outs of, the absolute true existence of, the unbelievably fabulous value of, the estate of Sir Francis Drake as now belonging to Oscar Hartzell.

This was typical:

I was going to get to the bottom of the whole matter and if I found out that George Drake was not the Proper Heir I was going to find out who was and this is Just what I done and my Powerful Friends obtained the assignment of the Proper Heir who Has been recognised by the Powers that be and the great Seals have been put on & has been boxed up beyond the reach of anyone except the officials that have the matter in charge as stated before. It took about Two Years to do that. Then the whole matter was brought before The Lord Chancellor and the Proper Heir that was living that assigned The Heritage to myself. It was all put in One Paragraph by itself. "His Majesty and those that represent His Majesty will deliver to the said Oscar Merrill Hartzell all the Monies, Title Deeds, all the Lands, Title Deeds, Monies and Personal Effects that belonged to Sir Francis Drake and his heirs." Now then, go right over again—"His Majesty and those who represent His Majesty will deliver at most possible speed all the Lands, Deeds, Title Deeds, Monies, Cumulations, and Personal Effects to the said Oscar Merrill Hartzell who becomes British subject and Sir Francis Drake at time of delivery." Now the Highest Seals of the United Kingdom are on that and she is Boxed Up by the Powers That Be, by the orders of the Powers That Be, and for any of the Officials that have the matter in Charge to divulge the transaction would be High Treason.

To read a page of this is dizzying; to read ten pages or more in similar vein is to conclude that Hartzell was unhinged, or spinning the most dazzling literary forgery, able to write mad as well as behave mad. Mangun came to the former conclusion, and I can only agree. Just when this happened, when, exactly, Hartzell lost his mind—that's another difficult matter. Mangun pointed to various moments in Hartzell's life—the death of his father, the bankruptcy, the move to England, the deportation, his arrest on the *Champlain*, the first trial, the development of severe diabetes in the early 1930s—and wrote that any of these crises might have assisted and accelerated a mental disintegration that certainly became more severe as time went on. Going crazy, after all, is often a process and not a stroke of the ax. I tend to think that the decisive moment in his disintegration was when Hartzell was brought back to America and faced thousands of his supporters demanding that he be who he'd been pretending to be. He couldn't face admitting that he wasn't, and so his personality split. Certainly, whether it was then or earlier, at some point Hartzell's dodging ceased to be artful and became deranged, and the insincerity of his performance began to transform itself into a passionate aria of madness.

Dr. Clark Mangun decided that Hartzell was "paranoid schizophrenic," a useful catchall diagnosis then becoming fashionable. He reported back to Judge Sullivan that Hartzell was indeed insane, and Sullivan dropped the case against him. So, if Hartzell had been acting, he got what he wanted, and would be eligible for parole in 1940. But now his future was in the hands of Clark Mangun, who had taken his measure and wasn't about to let parole happen. Oscar was staying put.

Mangun wrote:

Hartzell makes no effort to describe himself as a human being who lived and loved his fellow man. His descriptions of himself would be rather appropriate for a machine. He is without insight. With but a few cents to his name, he gives every evidence of living a happy existence. He believes himself to be worth 53 billion pounds sterling and to be possessed of a power approaching omnipotence. He has no appreciation that he is a diabetic old man who will probably never live to complete serving a ten year sentence in prison.

SEVEN

Finished but Not Ended

In the late 1930s, in the Muir Valley redwoods near San Francisco a piece of rusted metal was found, a brass plate or plaque, evidently some hundreds of years old. A fellow had been using it to block a hole beneath his feet in his car. On examination it was seen that the plaque had on it an inscription, writing that seemed to record Sir Francis Drake's annexation of what he had called New Albion when he touched land there during his circumnavigation of the globe in 1579. Local California opinion was divided on the question of whether the plaque was genuine. A metallurgist's report said it was, and this raised a question—did California belong to Sir Francis Drake and his heirs? Might even the whole of America?

People wrote to the State Department in Washington, asking if the discovery of the plaque was connected in any way with the shares they'd bought in a deal known as the Sir Francis Drake Estate. When these letters referred to the person handling the deal in America they mentioned not Oscar M. Hartzell but a woman based now in California, a woman named Sudie B. Whittaker.

Milo Lewis had long since ceased to be associated with the Drake scheme. He had married yet again, this time to a French woman, and he had been successful in a long campaign to be reinstated at the Illinois State Bar. Lewis was living in Paris, a devout Christian Scientist and well enough regarded by people at the American embassy for them to lobby on his behalf. But if Milo Lewis was now treading the straight and narrow, Sudie Whittaker most certainly hadn't reformed, but had pushed farther and farther west, peddling her version of the Drake scam. She'd never stopped working the con (and would disappear from the scene completely only with the advent of World War II), although she'd been forced to play second string to Hartzell for more than a decade. Now she came again to the forefront, and it's tempting to consider the possibility that she'd had a hand in her old enemy's downfall. Judge Graves was seen in Sioux City in 1933, remember, and around the same time the old indictment against Whittaker in Des Moines was dropped and struck from the record. Perhaps some bargaining went on. I also wonder if she might have been behind the anonymous postcards that became a central feature of the Scotland Yard investigation. If so, the revenge was no doubt relished.

In Iowa, Minnesota, and the Dakotas, Hartzell's bubble had at last been punctured; his balloon had been, to borrow his idea, "defined." People still clung to their receipts, but in their hearts hope was being replaced by the sad and bitter awareness that they'd been had. For a while, through 1936, letters continued to arrive at Springfield, insisting on Hartzell's innocence or questioning whether he was imprisoned at all. Soon these letters ceased, and his fame began to evaporate.

The man himself was mad but happy, undaunted. He progressed from janitorial duties to working in the hospital library, filling out cards and wheeling the book cart. The beginning of the war in Europe threw him into a fret, but he soon comforted himself with the assurance that this was another part of the grand scheme and he could put an end to the hostilities if he wanted to. One nurse noted: "He believes that when the U.S. flag is rolled down in the evening another is rolled up which states he is the ruler of the world." He still showed signs of mental sharpness, scoring a perfect 100 percent in his library test in February 1940 and cheerfully pointing out to a nurse the other inmates who were "in a fog"; then he congratulated this same nurse because she was the only one of the staff who was not a duplicate—he said he'd replaced all the others with members of his party.

Clark Mangun's only contact with Hartzell now was to note every year that he was too sick and mad for parole. Hartzell blew his Drake trumpets for the benefit of mere nurses and orderlies—if they'd spare him the time. When the name of Springfield was changed, from the Hospital for Defective Delinquents to the more seemly but less pungent Medical Center for Federal Prisoners, all the inmate numbers were altered too, a simple H being added rather than the previous DD. Hartzell heralded this as an acknowledgment of his power—the H stood for "Hartzellism." He said that the king of England had been at Springfield, taking pictures of him which had been published all over the world; he threatened to chop off the heads of all his enemies, including all the people who worked at the hospital—he had a machine that enabled him to chop off twenty thousand heads in one night, although his arms got tired working the lever. Probably this was routine for the Springfield staff. In March 1941 it was noted: "He has calmed down in the last few weeks. He no longer talks about flying to Mars or breaking up the Moon or even of the visits of the British Royal family."

He complained for months of a sore throat, of being unable to sleep because of a throbbing in his larynx. His throat was so tight that food sometimes wouldn't go down and came out through his nose. "This morning my throat broke like a cork coming out of a bottle—black blood and corruption, just like a boil," he told a nurse.

Looking through his daily medical reports in the Notorious Offenders file, I felt the blow coming. He had cancer of the throat, and a tracheotomy was performed on March 4, 1942. The next year was a grim struggle, a clinging to life. No visits, few letters: he sat in a wheelchair most of the time, staring out of the window toward the

Ozarks, slowly losing ground. Everyone at Springfield knew he was dying, and there was nothing they could do. The only food he could take was beef broth fed through a metal plate attached to the base of his throat. He lost weight, had trouble speaking, and blood and pus came out of the tracheotomy tube. A photograph from this time, the final photograph taken of him, shows a gaunt face with eyes staring into the camera lens as if to electrify or devour it.

"It is a hopeless case," noted Dr. H. A. Rasmussen on March 6, 1943, recommending that X-ray treatment stop.

A letter arrived from Des Moines. Penned in girlish handwriting and addressed to the Springfield governor, it said: "Don't want to cause you too much writing—but would like to know what Oscar's condition is now, if living. I do hope he's well. We were married once." The letter was signed Daisy Rees Fritz, Daisy Hartzell's name upon her second marriage. Even after everything, she cared for him.

At 12:55 p.m. on August 27, 1943, Hartzell collapsed in the bathroom and was carried back to his bed. His pulse was irregular, his skin cold and clammy. He died at 2:15 p.m. without regaining full consciousness. The cause was given as carcinoma of the larynx, with contributing diabetes. It was also thought that he might have had a terminal embolism of the brain.

Hartzell's sister, Pearl Palmer, made and paid for the funeral arrangements. She sent a telegram from her home in Galva, Illinois, refusing to allow an autopsy. Hartzell's corpse was shipped back by train to Monmouth and was entombed alongside his father and mother. A final list of his belongings showed what he had in his wallet and pockets at the time of death: ten cents. The $700,000 in Canada, the monies in various accounts in England, the $86,000 in Galva—these sums were never accounted for.

At first, on reading the brief account in Jay Robert Nash's *Hustlers and Con Men*, I was drawn to Hartzell's story because it was so enchanting, containing elements of the comic, the bizarre, the tragic, the almost incredible. It seemed to promise not only diversity of tone but a satisfyingly complete trajectory; it had, I thought, the possibility of a splendid picaresque. I was amazed, and am still, that the story was not better known. Although exception is made for really good murderers and serial killers, crooks on the whole aren't supposed to be the subjects of history, or biographies, which tend to get handed out like merit badges to those lives that society deems great and worthy. An irony of Hartzell's life was that he came wholly, and madly, to believe that he had lived in such a way—glorious, achieving, successful. He thought he was a hero, like Drake himself, whereas in fact he was an American antihero, a figure of fable or ballad. His exploits are salutary enough to satisfy even the strictest finger-wagger who wishes to warn of the calamity and doom that await those who embark on a life of crime. Yet they also sing a siren song to someone who, like me, sees in the confidence trickster an emblem of romantic individualism, and capitalism, gone astray.

Digging deeper, tracking the archive, doing interviews and research, following Hartzell's trail, I excavated more and more of a story that proved as haunting as it was extraordinary. Along with the unexpected twists and turns came shudders of recognition, reminders of my own father's struggles, his failures, achievements, and disappointments: the running away from home, the business boom and bust, the moving with a bad crowd, the furtive thrill of fashioning a new identity in a city far away, the cheating, the lying, the driven desire to escape oneself and slip into a more compelling role, the clusters of choices which direct life along a tightrope across a pit of disaster, into which one tips.

I recognized myself too, for I fear that I'm uncomfortably like

Hartzell at heart, on the run from the very thing which, no matter how often I change, how subtly or violently I shift my shape, will catch and expose me in the end. That thing, I suppose, is *who I am*— a crook, a fraud, an impostor. Many have this anxiety—they'll be found out in the end. Hence our fascination with the con man, who dances so nimbly and delightfully away from forces that nonetheless do at last tend to catch up with him. Long ago, in the late 1970s, around the time my father returned from his escapades, I went on my own binge of petty, and not so petty, crime: thieving, forging checks, breaking into houses. I'm not proud of any of it. Equally, I can't deny that just as those events were a product of what shaped me, so they've helped make me what I am now: someone with a precarious sense of his own balance and compass, someone magnetized by a story like Hartzell's. In writing about him I've sometimes had the feeling that I've been writing both a warning to myself and an incitement to riot. One side of me, thinking about him, says: watch yourself, be mindful of your choices and who you are and what you can do, above all find out what reality is and face it—know thyself. Worthwhile messages indeed, but then the other side of me, reveling in Hartzell's triumph over Milo Lewis, smiling at the business of the detective Mogford, wants to holler in appreciation. This duality informed and dictated the pattern of the quest as well as fueling it, for I'm a writer, and writers are tricksters and manipulators too (often benevolent and useful ones), calling into being real or unreal worlds which depend upon the artful arrangement of story, tone, and detail, upon the almost conspiratorial creation of an idea or dream for the reader to share, most especially upon the projection of that most winning of qualities, a quality the writer might rarely feel but struggles to evoke and then strives to make appear light and effortless—confidence.

In the years since 1943, Oscar Hartzell has been forgotten, although the essence of the Drake Estate swindle is still with us. "Thousands of Cubans are looking for pirate treasure," headlined the *Wall Street Journal* on April 20, 2001. The story described how fortune-seekers were obsessively questing for riches that the family of the Spanish corsair Andrés de Marco "hid from the Spanish crown in a London bank in the 18th century. Today their thousands of living heirs believe that with a couple of centuries of accrued interest their inheritance is worth hundreds of billions of dollars." Lawyers were at work in Cuba, and a familiar fever was spreading over the island as the hopefuls got ready to spend their money. It was the Drake scam, cooked up à la Castro.

Nor is the vision of sudden and transforming wealth persuasive these days only to the *misérables* of a strained Communist regime. Americans seem to be as giddy and vulnerable as ever. "Old money-laundering scam proliferating on the Internet," said the *Los Angeles Times* for August 27, 2001. This story was about "an old scam that promises to pay Americans millions to help Nigerian 'officials' smuggle cash and valuables out of their country." A U.S. Secret Service advisory noted that a large number of victims were being enticed into believing that they'd been singled out to share in multimillion-dollar windfalls in return for investing almost nothing. Again, it was Drake, and the memory of Oscar Hartzell lived on, this time in garb of deepest Africa.

Writing in *Scribner's Magazine* in the summer of 1935, Karl Crowley, the solicitor of the Post Office, reviewed the Drake scheme and asked: how gullible is the public? Crowley declared that the gullibility of the public was as yet unmeasured. "When we compel a swindler to show cause why he should not be deprived of the use of the mails, good citizens frequently berate the Post Office, either by letter, or in person, for 'persecuting' an 'honest man' who was just ready to bring poor mankind health or wealth, as case might be.'"

To get something for nothing never loses its appeal, Crowley concluded, and in hard times the lure of the Drake Estate defied newspaper exposures, the ridicule of leading state and government officials, fraud orders, arrests, trials, and convictions.

I think that the appeal of Drake's fortune went deeper still, drawing from the fathomless reservoir of America's need to believe, especially in the redemptive, almost religious powers of success and wealth. Optimism is America's oxygen, confidence its lifeblood, a continuing openness and even innocence two of its abiding features. By no means the worst thing that can be said of a country is that it produces a con man like Hartzell, for Hartzell, like any swindler, depended not just on greed but on qualities we know to be good. He was in every way a perfect candidate to become the figurehead of a deluded movement that grouped itself behind feelings of faith, trust, and an unreasoning preparedness to believe in the future's elusive beacon.

He had dreamed the dream more ferociously than anyone knew. In an interview with Clark Mangun, he said: "When this thing is all over, Lincoln nor any of them will have got anything on me about a cabin, nothing on me as a self-made man. It was a little three-room house and I've split rails. Better call it a shanty—more than anything else. Yes, Lincoln or any prominent man you've ever heard of has got nothing on me as far as starting at the bottom. I've had quite a career, Doctor."

ACKNOWLEDGMENTS
AND SOURCES

Many people gave generously of their time and assistance while I was writing this book. Some heard from me so often they had no choice but to become friends, and *Drake's Fortune* owes much to them.

Tim Rives, of the U.S. National Archives, Central Plains Region, in Kansas City, located the transcripts of Hartzell's Sioux City trial (which included an unpublished memoir by prosecutor Harry Reed) and helped me subsequently in so many ways I can't begin to thank him. His boss, Diana Duff (another Hartzell addict), inspired me with her enthusiasm for the story.

It was Linda Robertson, the librarian at the State Law Library of Iowa, who, while looking for the Sioux City transcripts, said to me, "We don't have those, but there are a number of bankruptcy trials involving a man named Oscar Hartzell twenty years earlier. Could this be the same fellow?" Thus opened a door into the whole section of the story that had never been looked at before—Oscar's career as a farmer, his involvement with Robert Moody, and his ruin in Madison County.

Another hugely lucky moment was when, having found a reference to Father Otto Zachmann, I called the Chamber of Commerce in Adrian, Minnesota, and was put in touch with Meredith Brody, the local librarian, who turned out to have done research on the still-lingering effects of the Drake Estate swindle in that part of the world. Meredith, herself a wonderful writer, was a paragon of generosity and diligence and dry humor, and I hope this book measures up to the unstinting help she gave.

Kim Walish, at the library in Sioux City, scoured the pages of the *Sioux City Journal* and the *Sioux City Tribune* and responded to my endlessly detailed inquiries with grace and patience.

Juleann Hornyack, clerk of the Supreme Court of Illinois, tracked down the documents concerning Milo Lewis's disbarment in 1922, unlocking another previously unopened door.

Kelly Hartzell kindly shared her own family history.

Rosie Springer, at the Iowa State Historical Society, supplied plentiful detail about the impact of the swindle in Des Moines and its surrounds.

In Madison County, Lorraine Kile tracked down court documents and Ted Gorman, publisher of the *Madisonian*, gave me excellent insights into the nature and mentality of that neighborhood.

Dr. Mortimer Ostaw gave me a vivid picture of life as a young psychiatrist at the Hospital for Federal Prisoners in Springfield, Missouri.

Roger Olien, from the University of Texas at Austin, generously shared his thoughts and knowledge concerning the amazing business scams of the indeed Roaring Twenties.

Richard Head, of the Metropolitan Police in London (no relation to the C17 rascal), told me of the existence of Hartzell's Scotland Yard file, warned me that it was closed under the Official Secrets Act, then steered me along the bureaucratic path to get it opened. Claudia Golden at the National Bureau of Economic

Research in Cambridge, Massachusetts, and Greg Clark at the University of California, Davis, helped me with the complex issue of historical monetary value.

No praise is too high for that historical resource known as the U.S. National Archives—bluntly, it's where a mouth-watering number of great stories reside. Fred Romanski made Hartzell's Notorious Offenders file available to me; Bill Creech and Aloha South sent the Post Office records; Milt Gustafson located State Department material; Glen Longacre tracked down the Chicago trial material.

Thanks to Molly McMinn of the U.S. Postal Service; Jeff Brody, curator of the National Postal Museum; Josephus Nelson, of the Manuscripts Division, Library of Congress; Linda Colton at the FBI; and the staffs of the UCLA Research Library, the UCLA Law Library, the Chicago Historical Society, the State Historical Society of Missouri, the New York Public Library, the British Museum Reading Room, the Scotland Yard museum, and the British National Public Records Office at Kew.

I mentioned that I first came upon the story of Oscar Hartzell in Jay Robert Nash's compendium *Hustlers and Con Men* (New York: Evans, 1976). Books in this area tend to be addictively entertaining, and other useful sources were:

Karl Abraham, "The History of an Impostor in the Light of Psychoanalytic Knowledge," in *Selected Papers* (London: Leonard & Virginia Woolf, 1927).

Herbert Asbury, *Sucker's Progress* (New York: Dodd, Mead, 1938).

Karl Baarslag, *Robbery by Mail* (New York: Farrar & Rinehart, c. 1938).

P. T. Barnum, *Struggles and Triumphs* (New York: American News Co., 1871).

Johannes Dietrich Bergmann, "The Original Confidence Man" (*American Quarterly* 21, Fall 1969).

John G. Blair, *The Confidence Man in Modern Fiction* (New York: Barnes & Noble, 1979).

W. T. Brannon, *"Yellow Kid" Weil: The Autobiography of America's Master Swindler* (Chicago: Ziff-Davis, 1948).

Robert Crichton, *The Great Impostor* (New York: Random House, 1959).

Arthur Lyon Cross, *Hartzell and the Mythical Billions of Sir Francis Drake* (Ann Arbor: *Michigan Alumnus Quarterly Review,* Winter 1937).

Joe Domanick, *Faking It in America* (Chicago: Contemporary Books, c. 1989).

Stephen Fay, Lewis Chester, and Magnus Linklater, *Hoax! The Inside Story of the Howard Hughes–Clifford Irving Affair* (New York: Viking, 1972).

Erving Goffman, *The Presentation of Self in Everyday Life* (Harmondsworth, England: Penguin, 1971).

Phyllis Greenacre, *Emotional Growth: Psychiatric Studies of the Gifted and a Great Variety of Other Individuals* (New York: International Universities Press, 1971).

Richard Head, *The English Rogue* (New York: Dodd, Mead, 1928).

Lewis Hyde, *Trickster Makes This World* (New York: Farrar, Straus & Giroux, 1998).

Clifford Irving, *Fake: The Story of Elmyr de Hory, the Greatest Art Forger of Our Time* (New York: McGraw-Hill 1969).

James F. Johnson as told to Floyd Miller, *The Man Who Sold the Eiffel Tower* (Garden City, N.Y.: Doubleday, 1961).

Alva Johnston, *The Legendary Mizners* (New York: Farrar, Straus & Young, 1953).

James Perry Johnston, *Grafters I Have Met* (Chicago: Thompson & Thomas, 1906).

E. J. Kahn, *Fraud*: *The United States Postal Inspection Service and Some of the Fools and Knaves It Has Known* (New York: Harper & Row, 1973).

Alexander Klein, *Grand Deception* (Philadelphia: Lippincott, 1955); *The Double Dealers* (Philadelphia: Lippincott, 1958).

A. J. Liebling, *The Telephone Booth Indian* (Garden City, N.Y.: Doubleday, Doran, 1942).

Gary Lindberg, *The Confidence Man in American Literature* (New York: Oxford, 1982).

Charles Mackay, *Extraordinary Popular Delusions and the Madness of Crowds* (New York: Random House, 1980).

St. Clair McKelway, *The Big Little Man from Brooklyn* (Boston: Houghton Mifflin, 1969).

David W. Maurer, *The Big Con* (Indianapolis: Bobbs Merrill, 1940).

Herman Melville, *The Confidence Man,* edited by Hershel Parker (New York: Norton, 1971).

Roger Olien and Diana Davids Olien, *Easy Money* (Chapel Hill: University of North Carolina Press, 1990).

The Reader's Digest Association, *Scoundrels & Scalawags: 51 Stories of the Most Fascinating Characters of Hoax and Fraud* (New York: The Reader's Digest Association, 1968).

A.J.A. Symons, *The Quest for Corvo* (New York: Macmillan, 1934).

Hugh Trevor-Roper, *Hermit of Peking* (New York: Knopf, 1977).

Warwick Wadlington, *The Confidence Game in American Literature* (Princeton, N.J.: Princeton University Press, 1975).

Charles R. Whitlock, *Chuck Whitlock's Scam School* (New York: Macmillan, 1997).

I referred to reportage in the *New York Times*, the *Times of London*, the *Los Angeles Times*, the *Kansas City Star*, and the *Chicago Tribune*, as well as many Iowa and Illinois newspapers. For material on Sir

Francis Drake I went to Garrett Mattingly, *The Armada* (Boston: Houghton Mifflin, 1959); Peter Padfield, *Armada* (Annapolis: Naval Institute Press, 1988); and James A. Williamson, *The Age of Drake*, 4th ed. (London: A. & C. Black, 1960).

Bill Thomas, my editor at Doubleday, first suggested the general area of confidence trickery as a topic, committed himself whole-heartedly to my choice of Hartzell as a specific case of lost history, and had inspired suggestions when it came to the text. Many thanks, Bill, co-conspirator. Thanks also to Kendra Harpster at Doubleday, to Bill Buford and Dorothy Wickenden at *The New Yorker*, and to Kyle Crichton, Brad Auerbach, Ric Burns, Andy Dowdy (con en-thusiast and proprietor of Other Times, the best used-book store in Los Angeles), and my friend and agent Jeff Posternak.

None of this would ever happen without my wife, Paivi Suvilehto.

All faults in *Drake's Fortune* are, of course, my own.

INDEX

Printed in the United States
by Baker & Taylor Publisher Services